From the reviews of *The Age of Consent*:

'Whether or not one shares his view of what is politically possible, *The Age of Consent* is a bracing challenge to the complacency of all varieties of establishment thinking. A veteran activist, Monbiot argues powerfully that protest is not enough. New thought is needed if real alternatives to prevailing power structures are to be found. Faced with capitalism in crisis, we must not retreat to the utopias of the past. With unsentimental lucidity, Monbiot demolishes the anarchist fantasy of a world without government. In practice, he observes, stateless societies leave the weak and the poor at the mercy of the strong and ruthless. He is equally brisk with the Marxist ideal of proletarian democracy, a utopian myth whose actual result is "a system doomed to sclerotic corruption". Monbiot's book is an arresting contribution to new thinking.'

Independent

'This book is rightly attracting attention, and raises issues that have long been neglected or deliberately buried. It should make people think; and as the author well says, if we do not like his ideas, then think of better ones. He believes that leaving things as they are is not a serious option. He makes his case.'
Financial Times

more reviews overleaf

'George Monbiot puts his political philosophy out front. He is interested in trying to articulate a road map to a better world, and offering an honest answer to that question which has been rendering the global justice movement hollow until now. He is superbly blunt about the failings of the movement so far: his dissection (and destruction) of anarchist arguments is the best I have ever read. It has become a boring social science cliché to say that we live in a world of rapid economic and cultural globalisation. Yet Monbiot upsets the low drone of sociologists with a series of rat-a-tat-tat demands: why should political globalisation be left out of the equation? Why is the nation state the sole unit within which democracy can exist? This is a weighty book that must be engaged with. At last, the global justice movement has found a vision as expansive and planet-wide as that of the American neoconservatives.'
Independent on Sunday

'The biggest single geopolitical issue today is the overweening power of the US in a unipolar world and the problem of how it should be handled by all other nations. No political leader can be said to have satisfactorily resolved this problem. George Monbiot's solution to the behemoth of growing world inequality in wealth and power is not tinkering with the existing institutions but replacing them wholesale. The key to his proposals is a return to the brilliant innovative insight of John Maynard Keynes in 1943 in preparation for the Bretton Woods conference, which determined the postwar international economic architecture that has prevailed ever since. Again, there is a breathtakingly radical sweep to all this. But before it is dismissed as the rabid fantasising of the Global Justice Movement, certain caveats are in order. This is not a whinge, but a very well argued statement of a positive alternative agenda. And if it is far too radical for some tastes, can they suggest any lesser options that will produce the same vast improvement in world justice and prosperity? The floor is theirs.'
MICHAEL MEACHER, *Guardian*

THE AGE OF CONSENT

A MANIFESTO FOR A NEW WORLD ORDER

GEORGE MONBIOT

HARPER PERENNIAL

Harper Perennial
An imprint of HarperCollins*Publishers*
77–85 Fulham Palace Road,
Hammersmith, London W6 8JB

www.harpercollins.co.uk/harperperennial

This edition published by Harper Perennial 2004
9 8 7 6 5 4 3 2 1

First published in Great Britain by Flamingo 2003

ISBN 0-00-715043-1

Set in Baskerville Classico

Printed and bound in Great Britain by
Clays Ltd, St Ives plc

I Angharad
Fy nghariad

ACKNOWLEDGEMENTS

My great thanks to Angharad Penrhyn Jones, Sandy Kennedy, Antony Harwood, Philip Gwyn Jones, Adrian Arbib, Zoe Broughton, Hugh Warwick, Hannah Scrase, James Robertson, Paul Kingsnorth, Kevin Watkins, Mark Lynas, George Marshall, Chris Grimshaw, Lisa and Gruff Penrhyn Jones, Amanda Jones, Kate Geary, Seumas Milne, Troy Davis, John Vidal, Paula Casal, the Tinkers' Bubble Trust, Terry MacDonald, Uri Gordon, Peter Haas, Eric Fern, Inez von Rège, Oliver Tickell, Jay Griffiths, Caspar Henderson, the Network Institute for Global Democratization, Nick Hildyard, Aubrey Meyer, Alastair McIntosh, Mike Schwarz, Brian Eno, Oliver Grant and Anthony Barnett.

Contents

Some Repulsive Proposals

Everything has been globalized except our consent. Democracy alone has been confined to the nation state. It stands at the national border, suitcase in hand, without a passport.

A handful of men in the richest nations use the global powers they have assumed to tell the rest of the world how to live. This book is an attempt to describe a world run on the principle by which those powerful men claim to govern: the principle of democracy. It is an attempt to replace our Age of Coercion with an Age of Consent.

I present in this manifesto a series of repulsive proposals, which will horrify all right thinking people. Many of them, at first sight or in conception, horrified me. I have sought to discover the means of introducing a new world order, in which the world's institutions are run by and for their people. Their discovery has obliged me first to re-examine the issues with which I have, for some years, been struggling. This process has forced me to recognize that some of the positions I have taken in the past have been wrong. It has brought me to see that the vast and messy coalition to which I belong, which is now widely known as the 'Global Justice Movement',* has misdiagnosed some aspects of the disease and, as a result, offered the wrong prescriptions.

In searching for the necessary conditions for an Age of Consent, I have not sought to be original. Where effective solutions have already been devised, I have adopted them, though in most cases I have felt the need to revise and develop the argument. Some of the policies I have chosen have a heritage of three thousand years. But where all the existing proposals appear to me to be inadequate, I have

---

* For several years, this movement was effectively nameless, though, for want of a better description, it was often characterized by the media and by some of its members as the 'Anti-Globalization Movement'. Most of its participants now reject this term. The name I've used has not been universally adopted: other people have called it the 'Civil Society Movement', the 'Anti-Capitalist Movement', the 'World Democracy Movement', the 'Alternative Globalization Movement' or the 'Movement of Movements'. This last term (and, for that matter, the diversity of the other terms) reflects its heterogeneous and perpetually shifting character. Some people have questioned whether it should be called a movement at all, suggesting instead that it be seen as a continuous series of incidental coalitions. The most accurate description might be 'a large number of people, dispersed among most of the nations of the world, who, in contesting the way the world is run, regard each other, most of the time, as allies'. For the sake of brevity, I'll continue to call it 'the movement'.

had to contrive new approaches. My principal innovation, I believe, has been to discover some of their synergistic effects and to start to devise what I hope is a coherent, self-reinforcing system, each of whose elements – political and economic – defends and enhances the others.

I have sought to suggest nothing that cannot be achieved with our own resources, starting from our current circumstances. Too many of the schemes some members of this movement have put forward appear to be designed for implementation by the people of another time or another planet. This is not to suggest that any of the transformations I propose will be easy. Any change worth fighting for will be hard to achieve; indeed if the struggle in which you are engaged is not difficult, you may be confident that it is not worthwhile, for you can be assured by that measure that those from whom you need to wrest power are not threatened by your efforts. We will know that our approach is working only when it is violently opposed.

Nor do I presume to suggest anything resembling a final or definitive world order. On the contrary, I hope that other people will refine, transform, and, if necessary, overthrow my proposals in favour of better ones. I have attempted to design a system which permits, indeed encourages, its own improvement, and mobilizes the collective genius unleashed whenever freely thinking people discuss an issue without constraint. And these proposals are, of course, a means to an end. If they fail to deliver global justice, they must be torn down and trampled, like so many failed proposals before them.

I will not explain them here, as this will encourage some readers to imagine that they have understood them and have no need to read on. I think it is fair to say that they and their implications cannot be understood in essence unless they are also understood in detail. The four principal projects are these: a democratically elected world parliament; a democratised United Nations General assembly, which captures the powers now vested in the Security Council; an International Clearing Union, which automatically discharges trade deficits and prevents the accumulation of debt; a Fair Trade Organization, which restrains the rich while emancipating the poor.

I have, I hope, made no proposal that depends for its success on the goodwill of the world's most powerful governments and institutions. Power is never surrendered voluntarily; if we want it, we must seize it. Because, for obvious reasons, the existing powers can be expected to resist such changes, they must be either bypassed or forced to comply. I believe, as the subsequent chapters will show, that I have discovered some cruel and unusual methods of destroying their resistance.

I ask just one thing of you – that you do not reject these proposals until you have better ones with which to replace them. It has been too easy for both our movement and its critics to dismiss the prescriptions they find disagreeable without proposing workable measures of their own, thereby preventing the possibility of radical change. If you believe that slogans are a substitute for policies, or that *if we all just love each other more, there'll be a transformation of consciousness and no one will ever oppress other people again*, then I am wasting your time, and so are you.

CHAPTER I

The Mutation

In his novel *Atomised*, Michel Houellebecq writes of the 'metaphysical mutations' which have changed the way the world's people think.

> Once a metaphysical mutation has arisen, it moves inexorably towards its logical conclusion. Heedlessly, it sweeps away economic and political systems, ethical considerations and social structures. No human agency can halt its progress – nothing, but another metaphysical mutation.[1]

These events are, as Houellebecq points out, rare in history. The emergence and diffusion of Christianity and Islam was one; the Enlightenment and the ascendancy of science another. I believe we may be on the verge of a new one.

Throughout history, human beings have been the loyalists of an exclusive community. They have always known, as if by instinct, who lies within and who lies without. Those who exist beyond the border are less human than those who exist within. Remorselessly, the unit of identity has grown, from the family to the pack, to the clan, the tribe, the nation. In every case the struggle between the smaller groups has been resolved only to begin a common struggle against another new federation.

Our loyalties have made us easy to manipulate. In the First World War, a few dozen aristocrats sent eight million men to die in the name of nationhood. The interests of the opposing armies were identical. Their soldiers would have been better served by overthrowing their generals and destroying the class which had started the war than by fighting each other, but their national identity overrode their class interest. The new mutation will force us to abandon nationhood, just as, in earlier epochs, we abandoned the barony and the clan. It will compel us to recognize the irrationality of the loyalties which set us apart. For the first time in history, we will see ourselves as a species.

Just as the consolidation of the Roman Empire created the necessary conditions for the propagation of Christianity, this mutation will be assisted by the forces which have cause to fear it. Corporate and financial globalization, designed and executed by a minority seeking to enhance its wealth and power, is compelling the people it oppresses to acknowl edge their commonality. Globalization is establishing a single, planetary class interest, as the same forces and the same institutions threaten the welfare of the people of all nations. It is ripping down the cultural and linguistic barriers which have divided us. By breaking the social bonds which sustained local communities, it destroys our geographical loyalties. Already, it has forced states to begin to relinquish nationhood, by building economic units – trading blocs – at the level of the continent or hemisphere.

Simultaneously, it has placed within our hands the weapons we require to overthrow the people who have engineered it and assert our common interest. By crushing the grand ideologies which divided the world, it has evacuated the political space in which a new, global politics can grow. By forcing governments to operate in the interests of capital, it has manufactured the disenchantment upon which all new politics must feed. Through the issue of endless debt, it has handed to the poor, if they but knew it, effective control of the world's financial systems. By expanding its own empire through new communication and transport networks, it has granted the world's people the means by which they can gather and coordinate their attack.

The global dictatorship of vested interests has created the means of its own destruction. But it has done more than that; it has begun to force a transformation of the scale on which we think, obliging us to recognize the planetary issues which bear on our parochial concerns. It impels us, moreover, to act upon that recognition. It has granted us the power to change the course of history.

Globalization has established the preconditions but this mutation cannot happen by itself. It needs to be catalysed, much as the early Christians catalysed the monotheistic mutation, or the heretical scientists the Enlightenment. It requires the active engagement of a network of insurrection-ists who are prepared to risk their lives to change the world. That network already exists. It forms part of the biggest global movement in history, whose members, most of whom inhabit the poor world, can now be counted in the tens of millions. The people of this sub-formation are perhaps not wholly aware of the project in which they are participating. They must seize this moment and become the catalyst for the new mutation. Like many catalysts, they risk destruction in the reaction, but if they do not strike, the opportunity created by their opponents will be lost.

The movement's defining debate is just beginning. Led by activists in the poor nations, most of its members have come to see that opposition to the existing world order is insufficient, and that its proposed alternatives will be effective only if they are global in scale. In searching for solutions to the problems it has long contested, it has raised its eyes from the national sphere, in which there is democ-racy but no choice, to the global sphere, in which there is choice but no democracy. It has correctly perceived that the world will not change until we seize control of global politics.

The quest for global solutions is difficult and divisive. Some members of this movement are deeply suspicious of all institutional power at the global level, fearing that it could never be held to account by the world's people. Others are concerned that a single set of universal prescriptions would threaten the diversity of dissent. A smaller faction has argued that all political programmes are oppressive: our task should not be to replace one form of power with another, but to replace all power with a magical essence called 'anti-power'.*

But most of the members of this movement are coming to recognize that if we propose solutions which can be effected only at the local or the national level, we remove ourselves from any meaningful role in solving precisely those problems which most concern us. Issues such as climate change, international debt, nuclear proliferation, war, peace and the balance of trade between nations can be

---

* In his book *Change the World Without Taking Power*, for example, John Holloway argues that a global revolution is dependent upon 'the realism of anti-power, or, better, the anti-realism of anti-power'. It will be achieved through 'flashes of lightning, which light up the sky and pierce the capitalist forms of social relations ... Think of an anti-politics of events rather than a politics of organisation.'[2]

addressed only globally or internationally. Without global measures and global institutions, it is impossible to see how we might distribute wealth from rich nations to poor ones, tax the mobile rich and their even more mobile money, control the shipment of toxic waste, sustain the ban on landmines, prevent the use of nuclear weapons, broker peace between nations or prevent powerful states from forcing weaker ones to trade on their terms. If we were to work only at the local level, we would leave these, the most critical of issues, for other people to tackle.

Global governance will take place whether we participate in it or not. Indeed, it must take place if the issues which concern us are not to be resolved by the brute force of the powerful. That the international institutions have been designed or captured by the dictatorship of vested interests is not an argument against the existence of international institutions, but a reason for overthrowing them and replacing them with our own. It is an argument for a global political system which holds power to account.

In the absence of an effective global politics, moreover, local solutions will always be undermined by communities of interest which do not share our vision. We might, for example, manage to persuade the people of the street in which we live to give up their cars in the hope of preventing climate change, but unless everyone, in all communities, either shares our politics or is bound by the same rules, we simply open new road space into which the neighbouring

communities can expand. We might declare our neighbour-
hood nuclear-free, but unless we are simultaneously working, at the international level, for the abandonment of
nuclear weapons, we can do nothing to prevent ourselves
and everyone else from being threatened by people who
are not as nice as we are. We would deprive ourselves, in
other words, of the power of restraint.

By first rebuilding the global politics, we establish the
political space in which our local alternatives can flourish.
If, by contrast, we were to leave the governance of the necessary global institutions to others, then those institutions will
pick off our local, even our national, solutions one by one.
There is little point in devising an alternative economic
policy for your nation, as Luís Inácio 'Lula' da Silva, now
president of Brazil, once advocated, if the International
Monetary Fund and the financial speculators have not first
been overthrown. There is little point in fighting to protect
a coral reef from local pollution, if nothing has been done
to prevent climate change from destroying the conditions
it requires for its survival.

While it is easy to unite a movement in opposition, it
is just as easy to divide one in proposition. This movement, in which Marxists, anarchists, statists, liberals, liber-
tarians, greens, conservatives, revolutionaries, reactionaries,
animists, Buddhists, Hindus, Christians and Muslims have
found a home, has buried its differences to fight its common
enemies. Those differences will re-emerge as it seeks to

coalesce around a common set of solutions. We have, so far, avoided this conflict by permitting ourselves to believe that we can pursue, simultaneously, hundreds of global proposals without dispersing our power. We have allowed ourselves to imagine that we can confront the consolidated power of our opponents with a jumble of contradictory ideas. While there is plainly a conflict between the coherence of the movement and the coherence of its proposals, and while the pursuit of a cogent political programme will alienate some of its participants, it is surely also true that once we have begun to present a mortal threat to the existing world order, we will attract supporters in far greater numbers even than those we have drawn so far.

The notion that power can be dissolved and replaced by something called 'anti-power' has some currency among anarchists in the rich world, but it is recognized as fabulous nonsense by most campaigners in the poor world, where the realities of power are keenly felt. Just because we do not flex our muscles does not mean that other people will not flex theirs. Power emerges wherever conflicting interests with unequal access to resources – whether material, political or psychological – clash. Within homogeneous groups of well-meaning people, especially those whose interests have not been plainly represented, it can be suppressed. But as any anarchist who has lived in a communal house knows, power relations begin to develop as soon as one member clearly delineates a need at variance with those of the others. The potential conflict is quelled only when one of the antagonists either buckles to the dominant will or leaves the community. Power, in other words, however subtly expressed, either forces the weaker person down or forces him out. Power is as intrinsic to human society as greed or fear: a world without power is a world without people. The question is not how we rid the world of power, but how the weak first reclaim that power and then hold it to account.

We must harness the power of globalization, and, pursuing its inexorable development, overthrow its institutions and replace them with our own. In doing so, we will, whether or not this is the intended outcome, bring forward the era in which humankind ceases to be bound by the irrational loyalties of nationhood.*

While we have hesitated to explain what we want, we have not been so shy in defining our complaints. The problem is simply formulated: there is, at the global level, no effective restraint of the ability of the rich and powerful to control the lives of the poor and weak. The United Nations, for

---

* I should point out that I see the 'Age of Consent' (my term for a world order which is responsive to the will of the world's people) as a precondition for the 'metaphysical mutation', not the mutation itself.

example, which is meant to deliver peace, human rights and international justice, is controlled by the five principal victors of the Second World War: the United States, the United Kingdom, Russia, France and China. These nations exercise the power of veto not only over the business of the UN Security Council, but also over substantial change within the entire organization.[3] This means that no constitutional measure which helps the weak will be adopted unless it also helps the strong.

The World Bank and the International Monetary Fund, which are supposed to assist impoverished nations to build and defend their economies, are run on the principle of one dollar, one vote. To pass a substantial resolution or to amend the way they operate requires an eighty-five per cent majority.[4] The United States alone, which possesses more than fifteen per cent of the stock in both organizations,[5] can block a resolution supported by every other member state. This means, in practice, that these two bodies will pursue only those policies in the developing world which are of benefit to the economy of the United States and the interests of its financial speculators, even when these conflict directly with the needs of the poor.

The World Trade Organization appears, at first sight, to be more democratic: every member nation has one vote. In reality, its principal decisions have been made during the 'Green Room' negotiations, which are convened and controlled by the European Union, the United States, Canada and Japan.[6] Developing nations can enter these talks only at their behest, and even then they are threatened if they offend the interests of the major powers. The result is that, despite their promises to the contrary, the nations and corporations of the rich world have been able to devise ever more elaborate trade protections, while the nations of the poor world have been forced to open their economies.

If you consider this distribution of power acceptable, that is your choice, but please do not call yourself a democrat. If you consider yourself a democrat, you must surely acknowledge the need for radical change.

Partly as a result of this dictatorship of vested interests, partly through corruption and misrule, and the inequality and destructiveness of an economic system which depends for its survival on the issue of endless debt, the prosperity perpetually promised by the rich world to the poor perpetually fails to materialize. Almost half the world's population lives on less than two dollars a day; one fifth on less than one. Despite a global surplus of food, 840 million people are officially classified as malnourished,[8] as they lack the money required to buy it.

One hundred million children are denied primary education.[9] One third of the people of the poor world die of preventable conditions such as infectious disease, complications in giving birth and malnutrition.[10] The same proportion has insufficient access to fresh water,[11] as a result of underinvestment, pollution and over-abstraction by commercial farms. Much of the farming in the poor world has been diverted from producing food for local people to feeding the livestock required to supply richer people with meat.* As a result of nutrient depletion, our continued survival depends upon increasing applications of fertilizer. The world's reserves of phosphate, without which most of the crops requiring artificial fertilizer cannot be grown, are likely to be exhausted before the end of the century.[13]

Climate change caused by emissions of carbon dioxide and other gases is further reducing the earth's capacity to feed itself, through the expansion of drought zones, rising sea levels and the shrinkage of glacier-fed rivers. Partly because of the influence of the oil industry, the rich world's governments have refused to agree to a reduction in the use of fossil fuels sufficient to arrest it.

The institutions founded 'to save succeeding generations from the scourge of war' have failed. Since the end of World War Two, some thirty million people have been killed in armed conflict. Most of them were civilians.

The world order designed by the rich and powerful has, unsurprisingly, been kind to them. The ten richest people on earth possessed in 2002 a combined wealth of $266

---

* The number of farm animals on earth has risen fivefold since 1950. They now outnumber humans by three to one.[12]

billion.[14] This is five times the annual flow of aid from rich nations to poor ones, and roughly sufficient to pay for all the United Nations' millennium health goals (such as halting and reversing the spread of AIDS, malaria and other infectious diseases, reducing infant mortality by two-thirds and maternal deaths in childbirth by three-quarters) between now and 2015.*

It would, of course, be wrong to blame only the states, corporations and institutions of the rich world for these injustices. There are plenty of brutal and repressive governments in the poor world – those of North Korea, Burma, Uzbekistan, Syria, Iraq, Turkey, Sudan, Algeria, Zimbabwe and Colombia for example – which have impoverished and threatened their people and destroyed their natural resources. But just as population growth is often incorrectly named as the leading cause of the world's environmental problems, for the obvious reason that it is the only environmental impact for which the poor can be blamed and the rich excused,† so the corruption and oppression of some of the governments of the poor world have been incorrectly

---

* Net Official Development Assistance to developing countries by members of the Development Assistance Committee is $53.7 billion. Estimates for the annual cost of meeting the millennium health goals vary from one agency to another, across a range of $20–25 billion.[15]

† This is not to deny that population growth exerts a major impact on the environment; but it is far surpassed by the rich world's consumption. A citizen of the United States, for example, consumes, on average, eighty-eight times as much energy as a citizen of Bangladesh.[16]

identified as the leading causes of its impoverishment. Zimbabwe's president, Robert Mugabe, is a brutal autocrat who has cheated his country of democracy, murdered political opponents and starved the people of regions controlled by the opposition. But the damage he has done to Africans is minor by comparison to that inflicted by the International Monetary Fund and World Bank, whose 'structural adjustment programmes' have been among the foremost impediments to the continent's development over the past twenty years.

Indeed, many of the countries we chastise for incompetent economic management are effectively controlled by the IMF. They are trapped by this body in a cycle of underinvestment. Because they do not possess good schools, hospitals and transport networks, their economic position continues to deteriorate, which in turn leaves them without the means of generating the money to supply these services. Yet they are prevented by the International Monetary Fund from increasing public spending, and forced instead to use their money to repay their debts. These are, as most financial analysts now concede, unpayable: despite a net transfer of natural wealth from the poor world to the rich world over the past 500 years, the poor are now deemed to owe the rich $2.5 trillion.[17] The IMF, working closely with the US Treasury and the commercial banks, uses the leverage provided by these debts to force the poor nations to remove their defences against the most predatory activities of financial speculators and foreign corporations. As Chapters 5 and 6 will show, there appears to be an inverse relationship between the extent to which nations have done as the international institutions have instructed and their economic welfare.

The effective control of many of the poor nations' economies by the IMF and the speculators, moreover, has dampened public faith in democracy: people know that there is little point in changing the government if you can't change its policies. The rich world, with a few exceptions, gets the poor world governments it deserves.

All these problems have been blamed on 'globalization', a term which has become so loose as to be almost meaningless; I have heard it used to describe everything from global terrorism to world music. But most people tend to refer to a number of simultaneous and connected processes. One is the removal of controls on the movement of capital, permitting investors and speculators to shift their assets into and out of economies as they please. Another is the removal of trade barriers, and the 'harmonization' of the rules which different nations imposed on the companies trading within their borders. A third, which both arose from and contributed to these other processes, is the growth of multinational corporations and their displacement of local and national businesses. There is no question that these processes have contributed to the power of capital and the corresponding loss of citizens' ability to shape their own lives. There is no question too that some of these processes have generated international debt, inequality and environmental destruction and precipitated the collapse of several previously healthy economies.

But, like many others, I have in the past lazily used 'globalization' as shorthand for the problems we contest, and 'internationalism' as shorthand for the way in which we need to contest them. Over the course of generations, both terms have acquired their own currency among dissident movements. While globalization has come to mean capital's escape from national controls, internationalism has come to mean unified action by citizens whose class interests transcend national borders. But perhaps it is time we rescued these terms from their friends. In some respects the world is suffering from a deficit of globalization, and a surfeit of internationalism.

Internationalism, if it means anything, surely implies interaction between *nations*. Globalization denotes interaction beyond nations, unmediated by the state. The powers of the United Nations General Assembly, for example, are delegated by nation states, so the only citizens' concerns it considers are those the nation states – however repressive, unaccountable or unrepresentative they may be – are prepared to discuss. The nation state acts as a barrier between us and the body charged with resolving many of the problems affecting us. The UN's problem is that *global* politics have been captured by nation states; that globalization, in other words, has been forced to give way to internationalism.

The World Trade Organization deals with an issue which is more obviously international in character – the rules governing trade between nations – and so its international structure is arguably more appropriate than that of the UN. But that issue is affected by forces, such as the circulation of capital and the strategies of transnational corporations, which are plainly global in character. Internationalism alone appears to be an inadequate mechanism, if one were sought, for restraining the destructive power of these forces. The global citizen, whose class interests extend beyond the state (and are seldom represented by the state), is left without influence over the way the global economy develops.

Globalization is not the problem. The problem is in fact the *release* from globalization which both economic agents and nation states have been able to negotiate. They have been able to operate so freely because the people of the world have no global means of restraining them. Our task is surely not to overthrow globalization, but to capture it, and to use it as a vehicle for humanity's first global democratic revolution.

CHAPTER 2

The Least-Worst System

An Equivocal Case for Democracy

I might appear to have begun with a presumption: that a democratic world order is better than any other kind. This was not the approach with which I started my research; I sought (perhaps not always successfully) to begin without preconceptions. I was forced to adopt this as my basic political model only after examining the alternatives, the two ideologies which, within the global justice movement, compete directly or indirectly with the package of political positions most people recognize as 'democracy' – Marxism and anarchism.*

---

* I am using 'democracy', 'Marxism' and 'anarchism' here as shorthand for a suite of economic and political positions. By 'democracy', I mean a form of government in which sovereign power belongs, in theory, to the people, in which those people have equal rights, and in which the will of the majority is expressed and exercised through elections between competing candidates and parties. I have used the terms

It is the common conceit of contemporary communists that their prescriptions have not failed; they have simply never been tried. Whenever it has been practised on a continental scale, the emancipation of the workers has been frustrated by tyrants, who corrupted Marx's ideology for their own ends. For some years, I believed this myself. But nothing is more persuasive of the hazards of Marx's political programme than *The Communist Manifesto*.[18] It seems to me that this treatise contains, in theoretical form, all the oppressions which were later visited on the people of communist nations. The problem with its political prescriptions is not that they have been corrupted, but that they have been rigidly applied. Stalin's politics and Mao's were far more Marxist than, for example, those of the compromised – and therefore more benign – governments of Cuba or the Indian state of Kerala.

'Marxism' and 'communism' to refer to the *political programme* laid out by Marx and Engels in *The Communist Manifesto*. I have treated 'anarchism' as self-government by autonomous communities of people who make their decisions directly, rather than by delegation, and which may or may not choose to associate politically or economically with other communities. I describe them here as if they are pure and distinct systems, whereas in practice each system may contain elements we associate with the others, as they may each incorporate answers to the different questions of who should rule, who should own the means of production and who should be permitted to use violence to resolve disputes. The package of measures we call 'democracy' has in fact benefited greatly from the thinking of Marxists and anarchists, and continues to evolve in response to the demands of its sceptics.

The *Manifesto*'s great innovation and great failure was the staggeringly simplistic theory into which it sought to force society. Dialectical materialism reduced humanity's complex social and political relations to a simple conflict between the 'bourgeoisie' and the 'proletariat'; that is to say the owners of property and the workers, by which Marx and Engels meant the industrial labourers employed by large capitalist concerns. Any class which did not conform to this dialectic was either, like the peasants, shopkeepers, artisans and aristocrats, destined to 'decay and finally disappear in the face of modern industry', or, like the unemployed, was to be regarded as 'social scum, that passively rotting mass thrown off by the lowest layers of old society',[19] with no legitimate existence in a post-revolutionary world.

Unfortunately for those living under communist regimes, society did not function as Marx suggested. The peasants, aristocrats, artisans and shopkeepers did not disappear of their own accord: they, like everyone else who did not fit conveniently into the industrial proletariat, had to be eliminated, as they interfered with the theoretical system Marx had imposed on society. Marx, who described them as 'reactionaries' trying 'to roll back the wheel of history', might have approved of their extermination. The 'social scum' of the *lumpenproletariat*, which came to include indigenous people, had to be disposed of just as hastily, in case they became, as Marx warned, 'the bribed tool of reactionary intrigue'. As the theory so woefully failed to fit society,

society had to be remodelled to fit the theory. And Marx provided the perfect excuse for ruthless extermination. By personalizing oppression as 'the bourgeoisie' he introduced the justification for numberless atrocities. The simplicity, of both the theory and the objective, is attractive and enticing. Even today, it is hard to read *The Communist Manifesto* without wanting to go out and shoot a member of the bourgeoisie, in the hope of obtaining freedom from oppression.

Moreover, Marx's industrial proletariat, modelled on the factory workers of Lancashire, upon whom he relied to foment revolution, turned out to be rather less inclined to revolt than the peasants, or, for that matter, the petty bourgeois, artisans, factory owners, aristocrats and educated middle classes from whom he drew almost all his early disciples. In order to overcome this inconvenience, Marx effectively re-invokes, in the form of bourgeois communist ideologues such as himself, the guardian-philosophers of Plato's dictatorship. Rather than trust the faceless proletariat to make its own decisions, he appoints these guardians to 'represent and take care of the future' of that class.

His prescriptions, in other words, flatly fail to address the critical political question, namely 'who guards the guards?' Democratic systems contain, in theory at least, certain safeguards, principally in the form of elections, designed to ensure that those who exercise power over society do so in its best interests. The government is supposed to entertain a healthy fear of its people, for the people are supposed to be permitted to dismiss their government. *The Communist Manifesto* offers no such defences. As the ancient Greeks discovered, guardian-philosophers tend rapidly to shed both the responsibilities of guardianship and the disinterested virtues of philosophy.

Moreover, by abolishing private property and centralizing 'all instruments of production in the hands of the State',[20] Marx granted communist governments a possibly unprecedented power over human life. Officials could decide what – indeed whether – people ate, where they lived, how they worked, even what they wore. Marx himself, in other words, devised the perfect preconditions for totalitarian dictatorship. The 'dictatorship of the proletariat'[21] transforms itself, with instant effect, into the dictatorship of the bureaucrat.

This problem is compounded by the Utopian myth at the heart of the *Manifesto*'s philosophy: that with the triumph of the proletariat, all conflict will come to an end, and everyone shall pursue, through 'the free development of each', 'the free development of all'. But history does not come to an end; dialectical materialism has no ultimate synthesis. New struggles do, and must, emerge as needs change, interests diverge and new forms of oppression manifest themselves, and a system which takes no account of this is a system doomed to sclerotic corruption. Indeed, Stalin and Mao recognized this, through their perpetual discovery of the new enemies required to sustain the dynamic of power.

Marx helped the industrial working class to recognize and act upon its power. His analysis remains an indispensable means of understanding both history and economics. But his political programme, as formulated in the *Manifesto*, was a dead end. It stands at odds with everything we in the global justice movement claim to value: human freedom, accountability, diversity. Any attempt to systematize people by means of a simple, let alone binary, code will founder, with disastrous consequences both for those forced to conform to the Marxist ideal, and for those judged by the all-powerful state to offend it.

At first sight, anarchism appears more compatible with the ideals of a global justice movement. It is the political idea I find most attractive, and to which, almost instinctively – however much I have now come to reject it intellectually – I keep returning. For the first few years in which I had a system of political beliefs, I considered myself an anarchist. Anarchism's purpose, of course, is to reclaim human freedom from the oppressive power of distant authority. Every atrocity committed by the state is a standing advertisement for self-government. Over the past one hundred years, as everyone knows, states have been responsible for the deaths of tens of millions of combatants and civilians in wars concocted principally for the purpose of expanding the wealth and power of the dominant elite. They have sought to destroy entire ethnic or religious groups: Jews, Roma, Tartars, Kurds, Tutsis, Bosnian Muslims, East Timorese, Maya,

Mapuches and many more. They have engineered famines, destroyed ecosystems, killed political opponents and curtailed the most basic human freedoms.

Those who have succeeded in capturing the wealth and power of the state have enriched themselves enormously at public expense: both King Leopold of Belgium and his indigenous successor Mobutu Sese Seko used the Congo as his personal treasury, effectively enslaving an entire nation for the purpose of filling his own pockets. The men and women who have governed all the recent superpowers – Britain, the USSR and the United States – have sought to enhance their power and secure domestic support without redistributing wealth, by seizing control of other nations and looting their economies. When anarchists assert that the state is a mechanism for violently depriving humankind of its freedom, we are forced to agree that it has repeatedly been used for this purpose. Anarchism, as a result, presents the most consistent – and within the global justice movement the most popular – challenge to the world order this manifesto invokes, in which governance plays a major role.

But the history of the past century, or even, for that matter, the past decade, is hardly an advertisement for statelessness either. When the government of Sierra Leone lost control of its territory, the lives of its people were ripped apart by men who are commonly described as 'rebels', but who possessed no policy or purpose other than to loot people's homes and monopolize the diamond trade. They evolved the elegant habit of hacking off the hands of the civilians they visited, not because this advanced any political or economic programme, but simply because no one was preventing them from doing so. Only when foreign states reasserted governance in Sierra Leone were the bandits defeated and relieved of their weapons.

When the state effectively collapsed in the former Soviet Union, losing its capacity to regulate and tax its citizens, the power vacuum was filled immediately, not by autonomous collectives of happy householders, but by the Mafia, which carved its empires out of other people's lives. The assets of the former state were seized not by the mass of its citizens, but by a few dozen kleptocrats. Anyone who sought to resist them was shot.

For most of the past decade, the eastern Congo has been effectively stateless, and the people who in earlier eras endured the depredations of King Leopold and President Mobutu, have been repeatedly attacked by six marauding armies and scores of unaffiliated militias, squabbling over their resources. Two million people have died as a result of this 'civil war'.

Anarchists would be quick to insist both that there is a difference between the stateless chaos of places like the eastern Congo and true anarchism (in which freely associating communities can seek mutual advantage through cooperation) and that many of the recent atrocities in stateless places were caused either by the collapse of the state or by the aggression of neighbouring states. We will turn to the first point in a moment, but it should surely be obvious that the second argument causes more problems for the anarchist position than it solves. Unless anarchism suddenly and simultaneously swept away all the world's states and then, by equally mysterious means, prevented new states from emerging, it is hard to see how the people of anarchist communities could survive when thrust into conflict or competition with a neighbouring state, which – by definition – would possess the wherewithal to raise an army. It is just as difficult to see how they could defend themselves from the robber barons arising within their own territories, who would perceive this collapse not as an opportunity to embrace their fellow humans in the spirit of love and reconciliation, but as an opportunity to embrace their undefended resources.

It is impossible to read any history, ancient or modern, without acquiring the unhappy intelligence that *Homo sapiens* is a species with an extraordinary capacity for violence and destruction, and that this capacity has been exercised in most epochs in all regions of the world. Those who wish to exert power over other people or to seize their resources appear to use violence as either a first or a last resort, unless this tendency is checked by some other force, principally the fear of punishment by people with greater means of violence at their disposal. Any political system which seeks to enhance human welfare must provide the means of containing and preventing the aggression with which some people would greet others.

The state claims to do so by asserting a monopoly of violence. By attesting that only the servants of the state are permitted to use violence against other people, and then only according to the rules the state lays down, it pretends to offer protection to its citizens both from external aggression and from people with violent tendencies within its own borders. In theory a democratic state is prevented, by accountability to its people, from the arbitrary use of that violent power against its own citizens. The notional safeguards against its use of violence towards the people of other nations are less clear-cut: indeed, this is among the global democratic deficits which this manifesto seeks to address.

In mature democracies, arbitrary violence by the state against its own people is fairly limited: the police sometimes beat up protesters and members of ethnic minorities and extort confessions from suspects by violent means, while the security services occasionally assassinate troublesome citizens. The anarchists would argue, with justice, that the relatively low frequency and low intensity of state violence in democratic nations reflects the fact that most citizens, most of the time, obey the state, whether they agree with its prescriptions or not. If people were more inclined to behave as they wished – in other words, if they were more free – they would be subject to a corresponding increase in state violence.

Nor will democratic states always succeed in protecting their own people from the violence of others. There is no shortage of recent examples of popular governments being deposed by external aggression. There are also plenty of instances of state authorities turning a blind eye while a faction with which they sympathize assaults a faction towards which they are antagonistic. Recent attacks on Muslims in India have been passively witnessed, and occasionally abetted, by police and soldiers. In Britain, as I know to my cost, the police often refuse to intervene when protesters are beaten up by private security guards.

But this system (with the significant caveat that it does not, as yet, prevent the state from attacking the people of other nations) does, at least, function in theory. It could be argued that both the state's own arbitrary violence and its toleration of the violence of certain favoured citizens are the results of the failure of its people to hold the authorities sufficiently to account. It is possible to see how, in a mature democratic state, effective campaigning by the victims of violence or their supporters could be turned into such a public embarrassment and electoral liability that the government is forced to desist. Indeed, on many occasions, precisely this has happened. There can, or so we should be inclined to hope, never be another Bloody Sunday in

Northern Ireland, or another sinking of a *Rainbow Warrior* by the French security services. Such restraint as democratic states display arises only from fear of losing public support, and therefore losing power.

No state but the dominant superpower can guarantee to defend its citizens from external aggression,* but the state does appear to be rather more capable of doing so – when it is responsive to the will of its people – than unaffiliated autonomous communities. Indeed, one of the reasons why both the Roman Empire and, 2000 years later, the British Empire, expanded so swiftly is that many of the tribes they attacked were either aggregated only loosely into states, or were not aggregated at all. Had there been no state of Nicaragua, the proxy warriors financed by the US could have overrun that region immediately, seizing the land and its resources from its people. The Sandinista government was far weaker than the United States, but, through ingenious organization, it succeeded in resisting the greater power for several years, during which it mustered the support both of other nations and of many people within the US. The eventual settlement was almost certainly less oppressive than it would have been, had the proxy warriors not encountered a regular army and the resistance and public relations coordinated by the state.

---

* And even the dominant superpower, as the attacks on New York and Washington in September 2001 showed, is not entirely immune.

It is not clear, by contrast, that anarchism works even in theory. The problem with the model is that, for the reasons outlined above, it has either to be applied universally, or applied only in those regions which are so poor in resources that no one else would want to live there. In other words, if states continue to exist, they will seize from relatively defenceless peoples the assets which would be to their advantage. Anarchist communities which possess valuable resources can sometimes survive for short periods in accessible places, or for longer periods in remote and impassable regions. Their establishment has often been associated with emancipation and, within the community, redistribution But these communities are always likely to be vulnerable to attack by those federations of people – which we call states – big enough to command armies and rich enough to deploy advanced military technology.

But let us suppose, as many anarchists do, that this system can, somehow, displace all states, simultaneously, worldwide. What we then discover is that this very universalism destroys the freedoms the anarchists wish to defend. Anarchists, like most people who support particular political systems, see those systems as responding to people rather like themselves. Most anarchists associate with oppressed communities, and envisage anarchism as the means by which the oppressed can free themselves from persecution. But if everyone is to be free from the coercive power of the state, then this must apply to the oppressors as well as the oppressed. The richest and most powerful communities on earth – be they geographical communities or communities of interest – will be as unrestrained by external forces as the poorest and weakest.

This is why, though both sides would furiously deny it, the outcome of both market fundamentalism and anarchism, if applied universally, is identical. The anarchists associate with the oppressed, the market fundamentalists with the oppressors, but by eliminating the state (as some, but by no means all the market fundamentalists wish to do), both simply remove such restraints as prevent the strong from crushing the weak. This, of course, is the point of market fundamentalism. But it is also the inevitable result of anarchism. If you have difficulty envisaging this, simply picture an autonomous community of impoverished black people living next to an autonomous community of well-armed white racists. For the majority of humankind to be free, we must restrain the freedom of those who would oppress us.

So the anarchists would have us make another extraordinary leap of faith. Having caused the state magically to evaporate everywhere, they also insist, without providing a convincing explanation of how this might happen in the absence of the state, that we can eliminate those disparities of wealth and power between communities which would permit one group of people to oppress another. But even that would prove inadequate. Even if every community had equal access to resources, there is nothing in the anarchist system to prevent one group from seeking to acquire more resources by invading another. Indeed, precisely this happens, almost continuously, among the nomadic tribes of that part of Africa where the borders of Sudan, Ethiopia, Uganda and Kenya meet. These are classic anarchist communities, with centuries of organizational experience, and far more sophisticated means of managing their resources and resolving disputes than the intentional communes of the West. They are forced into cooperation within the tribe by the erratic ecology of the lands they inhabit and their consequent inability to sustain the accumulation of wealth. They have been, by and large, abandoned by central government

Their loyalty to other members of the tribe is unimpeachable, but whenever the livestock belonging to another tribe come within range and are insufficiently defended, those men with sufficient arms will attempt to steal them. These forays, especially since the arrival of modern weapons, can be exceedingly bloody. When I was working with the Turkana of north-western Kenya, my visit to a cattle camp was delayed by illness. By the time I arrived, all that remained of its people were their skulls and the remains of their clothes, scattered across the savannah after their bodies had been eaten by hyaenas. Warriors from another tribe had arrived in the night, surrounded the camp, and inoculated it with bullets. Ninety-six of its ninety-eight people were killed.[22]

The anarchists may respond that the brotherhood of man has, in this case, been corrupted by modern weaponry.

There is no question that automatic weapons have accelerated conflict, but long before they first experienced the electrifying sensation of holding the stock of a gun, the people of these anarchist communities murdered their enemies when they perceived that they were favoured by the balance of power. Indeed another anarchist tribe, the Maasai, armed only with spears and knives, seized almost all the grazing lands of what is now central and southern Kenya and northern Tanzania within a century of emerging from the region the Turkana now inhabit. So the anarchists, as well as disposing of states, greed, wealth and power, would also need to disinvent all weapons which could be used to harm another person: not just bombs and automatic rifles, but also, as the massacres in Rwanda show, any bit of metal, stone or wood which can be sharpened on one side or knocked into a point. Theirs may be the perfect political system for another planet, inhabited by life-forms whose responses to scarcity and competition are the very opposite of ours. Regrettably, it is not a system destined to enhance the lives of those who live here.

The absence of government, then, is unworkable and ultimately intolerable. Communist government appears to depend on the extermination of entire categories of human being, while vesting power in the hands of unaccountable dictators. The dictatorship of vested interests, which is what passes for governance at the global level today, is oppressive and unjust. Unless some other system, which all political philosophers have so far overlooked, emerges, we are forced to conclude that all we have left is democracy.

Democracy is unattainable unless it is brokered by institutions, mandated by the people and made accountable to them, whose primary purpose is to prevent the strong from oppressing the weak and to prevent people of all stations from resolving their differences by means of violence. The collective noun for such institutions is government. So democratic government, of one kind or another, appears to be the least-worst system we can envisage. It is the unhappy lot of humankind that an attempt to develop a least-worst system emerges as the highest ideal for which we can strive. But if democracy is the only system which could deliver the Age of Consent we seek, we immediately meet a paradox. The reason why democratic governance is more likely to deliver justice than anarchism is that it possesses the capacity for coercion: the rich and powerful can be restrained, by the coercive measures of the state, from oppressing the rest of us.

This is not the only sense in which democracy compromises consent. In long-established democracies, no living person has volunteered her consent to the system under which she lives, for it pre-dates her. In some of the newer democracies, the majority of those of voting age alive today may well have supported the political system's formation, but those who are coming of age, and will also be forced to submit to the system, have not been consulted. Succeeding generations are likely to inherit the structures approved by their parents, whether or not they wish to be bound by them themselves. Of course, we can vote for reform and seek to persuade our representatives to change the constitution, but even in the most responsive of democratic systems, citizens are unlikely to be permitted to vote to dissolve the state, not least because so many powerful people have an interest in sustaining it. As Marx noted, 'Men make their own history, but not in circumstances of their own making.'[23]

A further problem is that, even if we do change the system, and a large majority approves of that change, there will always be people who do not. Yet they, just as much as everyone else, must surrender their consent and submit to the will of the majority. This is a distressing property of the democratic order: that it does not permit those who wish to remove themselves from the system to do so. But it appears to be a necessary one, if we are to prevent the powerful from escaping the legal restraints which defend us, however inadequately, from exploitation. This does not mean that we cannot break the rules with which we disagree. Indeed from time to time, many of us in the global justice movement violate the laws against criminal damage, obstruction or breach of the peace for political purposes, and believe we are morally justified in doing so. But the sustenance of the democratic state requires that we should expect it to seek to prevent us from doing so. We can, of course, use civil disobedience to try to change the law when, as it so often does, it discriminates in favour of the powerful. But without a body of law and the assumption of equality before it, the weak are without institutional defence.

In another sense, however, democracy is more consensual than any other political system, in that it is the only one which, in principle at least, consistently provides us with opportunities for *dissent*. It permits us to express our disapproval of policies and ideologies which offend us, to vote against them, and to overthrow them without bloodshed. No other system offers this. Orthodox Marxist regimes are viciously intolerant of dissenters. Anarchist systems appear to offer great scope for dissent within a community, as well as the opportunity to leave that community and join another one, but because they do not protect us from persecution, the only means of dissenting from the violence of others is through greater violence of our own. If we happen to possess the less effective weapons or belong to the smaller community, that dissent will be pointless. The dictatorship of vested interests offers opportunities for dissent only to those who represent the vested interests.

This is not to say that democracy is without substantial and systemic dangers. The most obvious of these is the tyranny of the majority. There have been plenty of states run by democratically elected governments which have, with majority consent, persecuted their minorities. The theoretical defences against this danger – such as weighted voting and special consultation rights – are flimsy and introduce problems of their own, such as *complexity* (rendering the political system less comprehensible and therefore less accountable) and *definition* (the laws designed to defend oppressed peoples can be exploited by oppressive minorities). But in this respect democracy appears to work rather better in practice than it does in theory. In most democratic countries, despite the recent advance of the far right, public acceptance of ethnic and religious minorities, homosexuals, children born out of wedlock and other oppressed groups appears to have increased with time. The same could not be said, for example, of the Muslim theocracies. Democracies whose people have access to communications technology appear to be self-improving in this respect, because they provide the political space in which minorities can explain themselves to the majority.

Another obvious danger is the crude and clumsy nature of the decision-making process. In representative systems, elections tend to be won or lost on just one or two issues, yet almost every party standing for election has dozens of policies. By choosing one potential government over another, we are forced to select an entire package, parts of which may be disagreeable to us. Representative systems permit a small degree of modification. If a political position turns out to be so offensive to the general will that it can threaten the survival of the government, it is likely to be dropped. But this is an insufficient safeguard, as most policies, though they may be particularly hurtful to a few people, or mildly hurtful to most people, are unlikely to generate sufficient opposition to threaten the entire government, especially if they are so complex that few will bother to discover what all their implications may be. This can be ameliorated a little by introducing an element of participatory democracy into a representative system, though this, as Chapter 4 shows, has its own limitations.

The third major problem with democracy is that a system capable of restraining the oppressor will also be capable of restraining the oppressed. If we are to prevent the rich and powerful from wrecking our lives, we require a government big enough to sit on them; but a government big enough to sit on them will also be big enough to sit on us. Conversely, if the system is sufficiently responsive to the will of the oppressed, it may also be responsive to the will of the oppressor. This, of course, is the great conflict at the heart of all democratic systems, and the one with which many of those in the movement have been rightly concerned. While states, over the past few years, have become ever more willing to regulate their citizens, they have become ever less willing to regulate the corporations. This is one of the problems this book seeks to address.

But while democracy has evident defects, it also possesses two great attributes. The first is that it is the only political system which contains the potential for its own improvement. We can overthrow our representatives without having to kill them. To a lesser extent, we can affect their behaviour while they remain in office. Democracy can be understood as a self-refining experiment in collective action.

The second is that democracy has the potential to be politically engaging. The more politically active citizens become, the more they are able to affect the way the state is run. The more success they encounter in changing the state, the more likely they are to remain politically active. Unhappily, this process appears to have gone into reverse in many democratic countries. As the competing parties offer ever less political choice (partly as a result of the constraints introduced by the migration of power to the global sphere), citizens are alienated from government, which leads, in turn, to a further withdrawal of the government from the people. A system which should be politically centripetal has instead become centrifugal.

The argument for democracy at the national level then seems to be – if not exactly robust – more compelling than the argument for any other system, or, for that matter, the absence of a system. But if we can – as most people do – agree that democracy is the best way to run a nation, it is hard to think of any reason why it should not be the best way to run the world. Indeed, it is surely demonstrable that many of the most pressing global and international problems arise from an absence of global and international democracy. The way in which states engage with each other is much closer to the anarchist model than the democratic one. The US government, like that of other superpowers before it, has seized the domestic mandate provided by its people (the 'autonomous community') to assert an international authority to rule the world. It expands its dominion – just like any powerful and well-armed community in the anarchist model – by means of violence and expropriation, in those parts of the world which do not form an alliance with it against lesser powers, succumb meekly to its demands, or successfully resist it with violence of their own. The democratic restraints within a state, in other words, do not prevent it from attacking weaker ones.

There are also, as this manifesto has argued, certain issues which affect humanity as a whole, and yet whose resolution is brokered by nation states. This introduces a number of problems. The first is that it permits powerful governments dominated by special interests to impose their will on the rest of the world. In some cases those governments are led by their domestic concerns to perceive a circumstance which is generally disastrous for humanity to be to their advantage. An administration which owes its election to the funds provided by oil companies, for example, will encourage the increasing use of fossil fuel.

The second problem with this brokerage of global issues by nation states is that even if all governments had an equal voice, our ability to affect their decisions is muted. Except in wartime, global and international issues seldom feature among the priorities of a domestic electorate. As national governments, we elect them, quite rightly, to tackle national issues. Without a separate process for determining what our response to a global issue may be, even a government with the best intentions has no effective means of assessing and representing the national will. This problem is commonly described as 'photocopy democracy'. A democratic decision is taken, to elect a particular government. That government then mandates an agency, such as a government depart- ment, to set certain policies. That agency then delegates people to represent those policies at the international level. With each 'copy', democracy becomes greyer and harder to decipher. This can be partly addressed through referenda, but the government still acts as a filter between us and the mediation of global policy. Moreover, we cannot guarantee that other governments would have polled their citizens. Governments which have consulted their people can be outvoted by governments which have not.

A third problem is that brokerage by nation states dimin- ishes the sense that we are all in this together. It encourages us to treat a problem affecting everyone on earth as a matter of national self-interest, and reduces our appreciation of our common humanity. Just as importantly, the lack of democ- racy at the global level leads to a lack of choice at the national level. National governments can seek to act as if they were free to respond to the will of their people, but they will be relentlessly dragged back to the set of policies imposed (by means I will explain in Chapters 4, 5 and 6) by those who possess global and international power. Without a global transformation, national transformations are impossible.

CHAPTER 3

A Global Democratic Revolution
The Case Against Hopeless Realism

Almost everyone who contests the way the world is run is at least vaguely aware of the problem of the migration of power to a realm in which there is no democratic control. Much of the effort of the democrats within the global justice movement has been devoted to addressing it. These people belong to two camps. The first consists of those who have sought to re-democratize politics by withdrawing them from the sphere (the global and international) in which there is no democracy and returning them to the sphere (the national and local) in which we appear to retain some political control. They see globalization as the problem, and believe that the re-invigoration of domestic democracy depends on its containment or reversal. The second consists of those who seek, by one means or another, to democratize globalization.

The most widespread and visible manifestation of the first approach is the strategy known as 'localization'. A book of this title has been published by the trade theorist Colin Hines.[24] His proposals, or something like them, have been adopted as policy by several national green parties. Hines points out that globalization forces workers in different countries into destructive competition, prevents nation states and citizens from controlling their own economies and helps the rich to become richer, while further impoverishing the poor. The trend of globalization, he suggests, should be 'reversed' by 'discriminating in favour of the local' by means of protectionist barriers. Imports should gradually be reduced, until every country produces 'as much of their food, goods and services as they can'. New trade rules must be introduced, forbidding states to 'pass laws . . . that diminish local control of industry and services', and a new investment treaty would ensure that countries are 'prohibited from treating foreign investors as favourably as domestic investors'.[25] All states would be forced by international law to introduce the same labour standards.

While some of the measures he proposes are, individually, arguable, his objectives are both contradictory and unjust. There is an argument for permitting the poorest nations to protect their economies against certain imports, in order to incubate their own industries. This, as Chapter 6 will show, was how almost all the countries which are rich today first developed. There is no argument founded on justice for permitting the rich nations to do so. If all nations were to protect their economies, the wealth of the rich ones might be diminished, but the poverty of the poor ones would not. We would, if we followed his prescriptions, lock the poor world into destitution. Trade is, at present, an ineffective means of transferring wealth between nations, but it has massive distributive potential; indeed, far more potential than an increased flow of aid, which reinforces the paternalism of the rich and the dependency of the poor, and which tends to be directed, anyway, towards those nations considered by the West to be of 'strategic importance'.

Colin Hines is in good company, however, because, though it pains me to say so, the approach of many of the most prominent members of the global justice movement in the rich world has been characterized by a staggering inconsistency. I once listened to a speaker demand, like Hines, a cessation of most forms of international trade, on the grounds of economic justice, and then, in answering a question from the audience, condemn the economic sanctions on Iraq. If we can accept – as almost everyone in the global justice movement appears to – that preventing trade with Iraq, or, for that matter, imposing a trade embargo on Cuba, impoverishes and in many cases threatens the lives of the people of those nations, we must also accept that a *global* cessation of most kinds of trade would have the same effect, but on a greater scale.

Many of the localizers have demanded measures which are the mirror image of those promoted by the market fundamentalists. While the fundamentalists insist that trade is the answer to everything, the localizers insist that trade is the answer to nothing. While the fundamentalists maintain that no economy should be protected, the localizers maintain that all economies should be protected. They have rightly condemned the fundamentalists' 'one-size-fits-all' approach, only to check it with a policy of equal coarseness.

But perhaps the most evident conflict within Colin Hines's prescriptions is that his formula for economic localization relies entirely upon enhanced political globalization. Nowhere in his book does he appear to address this point, or even to acknowledge it. His model requires draconian controls on the freedom of nation states to set their own economic policies, enforced by such global institutions as an Alternative Investment Code, a General Agreement for Sustainable Trade and, rather wonderfully, a 'World Localization Organization'. These would coordinate global controls on capital flows, taxes on financial speculation, global competition and exchange rate rules and debt forgiveness for the poorer nations. He offers no clues as to how this new kind of globalization might come about, how it might be rendered democratically accountable or how enhanced political cooperation could be sustained while nations cut their economic ties. All these new global measures, needless to say, are to be accompanied by the 'maximum devolution of political power' and the surrender of 'control of the local economy to the locality'.[26]

There is another means of reclaiming power from globalization greatly favoured by theorists within this movement, and that is to bypass governments and the usual political processes, and seek to shape global futures directly, by changing the decisions which govern the daily pattern of our lives. In his beautifully written book *The Post-Corporate World*,[27] the development economist David Korten acknowledges the need for political campaigning and global measures to redistribute power and wealth, but he seeks to contest the power of transnational corporations principally by changing the behaviour of those who work for them, buy their products and own their stock. Through 'mindful living' we can free ourselves 'from the imposed order of coercive institutions that constrain life's creative power ... To be truly free we must learn to practice a mindful self-restraint in the use of our freedom.' His prescriptions could be summarized as 'consumer democracy', 'shareholder democracy' and 'voluntary simplicity'.

Consumer democracy means, in Korten's words, that, 'in good market fashion, you are voting with your dollars'. By 'starving the capitalist economy', you can 'nurture the mindful market'.[28] By using your money carefully, in other words, you can help to create a world in which other people are not exploited and the environment is not destroyed.

None but the market fundamentalists would deny that there is a moral imperative to spend our money carefully. If we believe that slavery is wrong, we should be careful not to help those businesses which depend on slavery to survive. If we wish to protect the Amazon rainforest, we should withhold from buying mahogany, whose extraction, in some parts of the Amazon, has activated other forms of destruction. But mindful consumption is a weak and diffuse means of changing the world, and it has been greatly overemphasized by those (though David Korten is not among them) who wish to avoid the necessary political conflicts.

The first and most obvious problem with consumer democracy is that some people have more votes than others. Those with the most votes – that is to say, with the most money – are the least likely to wish to change an economic system which has served them well. If we reject the one-dollar, one-vote arrangement which determines the way the World Bank and IMF are run, on the grounds that this is a grossly unjust means of resolving political issues, we should surely also reject a formula for changing the world which relies on the goodwill of those with the most dollars to spend. It should be obvious that the decisions made, in this weighted voting system, by the people with the most money will not, in aggregate, be decisions made in the interests of those with the least.

Those who do seek to make ethical purchasing decisions will often discover, moreover, that the signal they are trying to send becomes lost in the general market noise. I might reject one brand of biscuits and buy another, on the grounds that the second one was less wastefully packaged, but unless I go to the trouble of explaining that decision to the biscuit manufacturer I chose not to patronize, the company will have no means of discovering why I made it, or even that I made a decision at all. Even if I do, my choice is likely to be ineffective unless it is coordinated with the choices of hundreds (or, depending on the size of the company, thousands) of other consumers. But consumer boycotts are notoriously hard to sustain. Shoppers are, more often than not, tired, distracted and drowning in information and conflicting claims. Campaigning organizations report that a maximum of one or two commercial boycotts per nation per year is likely to be effective; beyond that, customer power becomes too diffuse. For the majority of products, therefore, the consumer's power of restraint is limited.

This problem is compounded by the fact that nearly everything we buy has already been bought at least once by the time it reaches us. Take, for example, the market for copper. I object to the way the indigenous people of West Papua, in Indonesia, have been treated by the operators of the massive copper mine at Tembagapura. Many hundreds of people have been forcibly evicted from their lands; Indonesian soldiers protecting the operation have tortured and murdered hundreds more; and the 'tailings' from the mine have damaged the fisheries which provided a critical source of protein for thousands of others. I would like that mine either to cease operating altogether or to operate only with the consent of local people. But I buy none of the copper I use directly. Most of it has been brought into my house by plumbers and electricians, or in the form of components – largely invisible to me – of electrical equipment. I have purchased it, in other words, as part of a package of goods and services, for which I have paid a single price. My leverage over the copper market then depends on the transmission of my will through a number of intermediaries. If I am prepared to embarrass myself, I might be able to persuade the electrician to go back to his company and ask it to question its suppliers, who in turn might be persuaded to approach the manufacturers who in turn might be persuaded to petition the mining company to discover whether or not the copper he is about to use in my house was produced with the consent of local people and without damaging the environment.

Even if this request is somehow transmitted all the way there and all the way back, and the electrician has not walked away from the job in disgust, all I am likely to receive is an unverifiable assurance that of course it was mined sustainably. I will be left feeling like a busybody and a supplicant, which is hardly a politically empowering position to be in. And I will be no nearer than I was before to closing down the mine at Tembagapura or altering the way it operates.

Of course, there are several organizations, such as the Soil Association and the Forest Stewardship Council, whose purpose is to bypass the purchasing chain, and determine directly, on our behalf, whether or not certain products (food and timber in these cases) are as eco-friendly as they claim to be, enabling the consumer to make an informed choice simply by checking the label. But important as these bodies are, their impact is limited by the constraint afflicting all consumer democrats: namely that they possess no negative power. I can congratulate myself for not buying cocoa produced by slaves, but my purchases of fairly traded chocolate do not help me to bring the slave trade to an end, because they don't prevent other people from buying chocolate whose production relies on slavery. This is not to say that voluntary fair trade is pointless – it has distributed wealth to impoverished people – simply that, while it encourages good practice, it does not discourage bad practice.

If we wish to prevent exploitation, it surely makes more sense to start at the other end of the purchasing chain, the end at which the exploitation takes place. If local people want to close the mine at Tembagapura, then let us campaign to help them to close it, so that we no longer have to fret about whether or not the copper we are buying is produced there. This is the means by which, for example, Western corporations were forced out of Burma, mahogany logging was brought to an end in Brazil and the biotechnology giant Monsanto was, temporarily, fettered. Consumer democracy is much less effective at reaching the source of the problem than plain democracy. An over-reliance on consumer democracy disperses our power. It permits us to feel we are making a difference when we are doing no such thing. It individualizes our political action when it should be consolidated.

There is rather more to be said for 'shareholder democracy', for while it suffers from most of the drawbacks of consumer democracy, it automatically collectivizes the power of the mindful purchasers, for every year the company's annual general meeting draws these people together, where they can coordinate their concerns. Campaigners buying the shares of companies whose practices they deplore have been devastatingly effective on such occasions, but only when their protests at these meetings are part of a wider campaign designed to damage the company's reputation.

'Voluntary simplicity' is defined by David Korten as 'spending less time working for money, leading lives less cluttered by stuff, and spending more time living'.[29] These are worthy aims (though they can be pursued only by the rich), but it is not clear that they translate into political change.

Korten celebrates the lives of people who have withdrawn their labour from destructive corporations, found less stressful employment and now spend more of their time engaged in the business of living. Many of these people, he suggests, will use this extra time to campaign for a better world. It is certainly true to say that it is hard to be an effective campaigner if paid employment consumes most of your time and energy. It is also true that there is an urgent need for all wealthy consumers to reduce their impact on the planet. But Korten, like many others, has exaggerated the transformative impact of this proposal.

In political terms, the aggregate effect of voluntary simplicity is merely an acceleration of the employment cycle. Instead of waiting until they are sixty or sixty-five before retiring from corporate life, more people are doing so in early middle age. They are not bringing the system to its knees by this means; they are simply making way for younger, keener, more aggressive workers. Far from threatening corporate power, this could enhance it, as younger workers are often easier to manipulate and less aware of the impact of their activities. The withdrawal of our labour from the corporations will hurt them as a sector only if everyone does it, all at once, by means of a worldwide, indefinite general strike. Again we run into the problem here that those who would be most inclined to strike are those with the least investment in corporate life.

Nor does it follow that, once people have left corporate employment, they will use their time to fight the forces which have supplied them with the savings or the pensions required to sustain their 'simplified' lives. Indeed, the two professed aims of voluntary simplicity – seeking an easier, less cluttered life and devoting more time to political campaigning – are starkly contradictory. If we are to exert any meaningful impact on the way the world is run, we need to engage in voluntary complexity.

'Consumer democracy' and 'voluntary simplicity' are easy and painless for their practitioners. We should, as I have suggested, be deeply suspicious of easy and painless solutions, for this suggests that such strategies are unopposed. A serious attempt to change the world will be difficult and dangerous. What appears to be a solution, in other words, may in fact be a withdrawal. Voluntary simplicity looks more like the monastery than the barricade. Delightful as it may be for those who practise it, quiet contemplation does not rattle the cages of power.

If an attempt to replace the global economy with a local economy locks the poor world into poverty, while fudging the issue of political power, and if consumer democracy and voluntary simplicity avoid power rather than confronting it, then our attempts to re-democratize the world by withdrawing from globalization appear to be doomed. This leaves us, as most of the movement now recognizes, with just one remaining option: we must democratize globalization. But even here we encounter another great division, this time between the reformists and the revolutionaries. While the revolutionaries wish to sweep away the existing global and international institutions, reformists such as the financier and author of the manifesto *On Globalization*,[30] George Soros, prefer to work within them.

Soros proposes certain measures, such as using Special Drawing Rights (the financial reserves issued by the IMF) to fund aid for poorer nations, changing the way the IMF intervenes in the economies of the poor world and giving the directors of the World Bank independence from the governments which appointed them. These are, as far as they go, progressive measures. But this, Soros insists, is the limit of what we can expect to achieve. 'It would be unrealistic', he argues, 'to advocate a wholesale change in the prevailing structure of the international financial system . . . the United States is not going to abdicate its position . . . I do not see any point in proposing more radical solutions when the authorities are not ready to consider even the moderate ones outlined here.'[31] Like many other people, George Soros regards the revolutionary alternatives as hopelessly unrealistic.

If we are to confine our proposals to what 'the authorities are ready to consider' then it seems to me that we may as well give up and leave the authorities to run the world unmolested. Even the modest reforms of the IMF and World Bank that George Soros proposes are blocked by the very constitutions with which he wishes to tinker. The United States has, as we have seen, a veto over any constitutional changes within these organizations. It has, at present, no incentive to drop this veto, and Soros offers no proposals to change the incentive. As a result, these bodies are constitutionally unreformable.

Another way of looking at the problem is this. Let us assume that through discovering some new incentives (and, as this book shows, there are one or two we could drum up) with which we might alter the behaviour of the United States, we can muster sufficient political pressure to persuade that nation to suspend its veto and permit the constitution of the World Bank and the IMF to be changed. We would then have forced the world's only superpower to have volunteered to surrender its hegemonic status. If that is possible, anything is. And if anything is possible, why on earth should we settle for the kind of reforms which Soros admits are 'puny when compared with the magnitude of the problems they are supposed to resolve'?[32] Why not embrace those proposals which give us what we want, rather than just what we imagine 'the authorities are ready to consider'?

George Soros's 'realistic' measures turn out to be either hopelessly unrealistic or hopelessly unambitious. Certainly, as he acknowledges, they provide no realistic means of solving the world's problems, even if they were implemented. Perhaps it would be more accurate to describe such proposals as 'hopelessly realistic'. They are hopeless in two respects: the first is that they are a useless means of achieving change, the second is that they reflect an absence of hope.

Just as importantly, compromised solutions will not command popular enthusiasm. Who wants to fight, perhaps *in extremis* lay down her life, for solutions which are 'puny when compared with the magnitude of the problems they are supposed to resolve'? We know that the reform of illegitimate institutions is likely only to enhance their credibility, and thus the scope of their illegitimate powers. No solution of any value to the oppressed will surface unless vast numbers of people demand it, not just once, but consistently, and they will not, of course, demand it if they perceive that it is hopeless.

Had those people who campaigned for national democratization in the nineteenth century in Europe approached their task with the same hopeless realism as the reformists campaigning for global democratization today, they would have argued that, as the authorities were not ready to consider granting the universal franchise, they should settle for a 'realistic' option instead, and their descendants might today have been left with a situation in which all those earning, say, $50,000 a year or possessing twenty acres of land were permitted to vote, but those with less remained disenfranchised.

Every revolution could have been – indeed almost certainly was – described as 'unrealistic' just a few years before it happened. The American Revolution, the French Revolution, female enfranchisement, the rise of communism, the fall of communism, the aspirations of decolonization movements all over the world were mocked by those reformists who believed that the best we could hope for was to tinker with existing institutions and beg some small remission from the dominant powers. Had you announced, in 1985, that within five years men and women with sledge-hammers would be knocking down the Berlin Wall, the world would have laughed in your face. All of these movements, like our global democratic revolution, depended for their success on mass mobilization and political will. Without these components, they were impossible. With them, they were unstoppable.

What is realistic is what happens. The moment we make it happen, it becomes realistic. As the other possibilities fall away, a global democratic revolution is, in both senses, the only realistic option we have. It is the only strategy which could deliver us from the global dictatorship of vested interests. It is the only strategy that is likely to succeed. We have responded to the Age of Coercion with an Age of Dissent. This is the beginning, not the end, of our battle. It is time to invoke the Age of Consent.

CHAPTER 4

We the Peoples

Building a World Parliament

Our global revolution requires no tumbrils, no guillotines, no unmarked graves; no revanchist running dogs need be put against the wall. We have within our hands already the means to a peaceful, democratic transformation. These means arise inexorably from an analysis of how the world is run, and why the existing world order fails. Each of the following three chapters examines one aspect of global governance, shows why the current system is not working, considers the possible alternatives, chooses those which seem to work best and then explains how we – the dissidents of the rich world and the citizens of the poor world – can, using only those resources available to us, replace the system which works for the powerful with one which works for the weak. The first of these tasks is perhaps the most pressing: altering the mediation of war and peace and the relations between nation states, and seeking to replace a world order built on coercion with one which emerges from below, built upon democracy.

The United Nations was conceived in 1941 by the United States, the United Kingdom and the Soviet Union, as an alliance against the Axis powers. As the Second World War progressed, its scope and membership expanded, until, in June 1945, fifty nations signed a declaration of principles – the United Nations Charter – whose purpose was to promote peace, human rights and international law, to encourage social progress and higher living standards and to prevent another World War.[33] The UN, in other words, was founded with the best of intentions. But these, like the motives surrounding every aspect of the postwar settlement, were mixed with some rather less elevated concerns. No one gives power away, and those nations which constructed the UN were careful to ensure that it reinforced rather than diminished their global pre-eminence.

This concern is reflected in the constitution of the supreme international body, which is charged with the prevention of war, the United Nations Security Council. If one nation is threatening or attacking another, the council may use whatever measures are necessary to force it to desist: it can order a ceasefire, for example; levy economic sanctions; send in peacekeepers; or, at the last resort, authorize the armed forces of the UN's member states to take military action against the aggressor. At the international level it asserts (though with little success) what the state asserts at the national level: a monopoly of violence.

The Security Council mimics the notional constraints of the democratic state. By this means it claims to sustain a world order founded on right rather than might. The problem with the postwar settlement is that those with the might decide what is right.

There are fifteen members of the council, of which ten have temporary seats (held for two years and then passed to another state) and five have permanent seats. Each of the five permanent members has the power of veto. no decision can be taken by the Security Council unless all five have approved it. Unsurprisingly, the five permanent members are the three powers which founded the United Nations – the United States, United Kingdom and Russia – and their principal wartime allies, China and France.* They granted themselves the ability to determine, for as long as the UN continues to exist, who is the aggressor and who the aggressed.

The power of veto was introduced partly in order to prevent those states in possession of nuclear weapons from

---

* Russia acquired the seat formerly occupied by the Soviet Union. China's seat was, following the revolution, held by Taiwan (the Republic of China) until 1971, when it reverted to the *People's* Republic (mainland China).

attacking each other: had the other member states, for example, collectively decided that the Soviet Union was threatening one of its neighbours, and then sought to restrain it through military action, the USSR may have responded by offering to meet that force with greater force, provoking another world war. Indeed, during the Cold War the Soviet Union used its veto repeatedly, precisely in order to prevent the other states from restricting its attempts to expand its imperial domain. But, while the veto may have functioned as a safety valve, preserving a global peace at the expense of the weaker states being threatened or attacked by one of the permanent members, it has also proved to be an instant recipe for the abuse of power and the impediment of justice.

The problem with the way the Security Council has been established is that those who possess power cannot be held to account by those who do not. The key democratic question – who guards the guards? – has been left unanswered. The Security Council is, by definition, tyrannical. Those who defend the way the world is run point out that veto powers have rarely been used since the end of the Cold War* and that the veto can, in theory, be deployed (as France and Russia tried to deploy it in 2003) to protect

---

* They have been used on eleven occasions between 1990 and 2001. Six of these were US vetoes on resolutions restraining Israel's treatment of the Palestinians.[34]

states from unauthorized attacks by other members; but the truth is that the threat of the veto informs every decision the Security Council does or does not make. Other member states know perfectly well, for example, that there is no point in preparing a resolution which the United States will reject. The US, and to a lesser extent the other permanent members, assert their will without even having to ask.

As other nations cannot hold them to account, the permanent members (or, more precisely, the two permanent members which have, since the UN's formation, wielded real power) can blithely defy every principle the United Nations was established to defend. Since 1945, the United States has launched over 200 armed operations,[35] most of which were intended not to promote world peace but to further its own political or economic interests. The Soviet Union repeatedly used its veto to prevent other member states from interfering with its sponsorship of violent insurrection, and occasional direct invasion. The five permanent members also happen to be the world's five biggest arms dealers, indirectly responsible for exacerbating many of the conflicts the Security Council is supposed to prevent. The five nations which possess the exclusive power to decide how threats should be handled are the five nations which present the gravest threat to the rest of the world.

The problem is compounded – and this is not commonly understood – by the fact that the powers of the Security

Council are not confined to the administration of peace. The UN Charter also grants the five permanent members vetoes over constitutional reform of the United Nations.* Even if every other member of the General Assembly votes to change the way the institution works, their decision can be overruled by a single permanent member. Any one of the five can also block the appointment of the UN Secretary-General,† the election of judges to the International Court of Justice, and the admission of a new member to the United Nations.[36]

Those who benefit from this system argue that it simply reflects the realities of power: if the five permanent members were not using their vetoes to force other states to do as they bid, they would find some other means. This is undoubtedly true; but the problem with the way the council is established is that, rather than moderating the realities of power, it compounds them. It offers an immediate and painless means for a permanent member to prevent the rest of the world from pursuing peace or justice, whenever it suits its interests to do so. These special powers have rendered the UN General Assembly, in which every member state has an equal vote, all but irrelevant. The 186 member states which do not occupy permanent seats on

---

* In Articles 108 and 109.
† In 1996, for example, the US blocked the reappointment of Boutros Boutros-Ghali.

the Security Council can huff and puff about how the world should be run, in the certain knowledge that real power lies elsewhere.

But even if the Security Council were to be disbanded tomorrow, and the supreme powers it possessed vested instead in the Assembly, the United Nations would still be far from democratic. Many of the member states are not themselves democracies, and have a weak claim to represent the interests of their people. Even those governments which have come to power by means of election seldom canvass the opinion of their citizens before deciding how to cast their vote in international assemblies. There is, partly as a result, little sense of public ownership of the General Assembly or the decisions it makes. At public meetings, I have often asked members of the audience to raise their hands if they know the name of their country's ambassador to the United Nations. Seldom, even at gatherings of the most politically active people, do more than two or three per cent claim to know; on one occasion an audience of 600 mostly well-read, middle-class people (it was a literary festival) failed to produce a single respondent. In turn, many of the ambassadors, who are appointed, not elected, appear to be rather more conscious of the concerns of their nations' security services than those of the citizens whose part they are supposed to take.

The assembly, too, is riddled with rotten boroughs. It is widely recognized in the United States that there is something wrong with a system in which the 500,000 people of Wyoming can elect the same number of representatives to the Senate as the thirty-five million of California. Yet, in the UN General Assembly, the 10,000 people of the Pacific island of Tuvalu possess the same representation as the one billion people of India. Their per capita vote, in other words, is weighted 100,000-fold. If the assembly had real powers, this inequity would be a major liability: in international bodies which do make real decisions, such as the Organization for the Prohibition of Chemical Weapons and the International Whaling Commission, rich and powerful nations bribe and blackmail small and weak ones to obtain the votes they need.[37]

But even if all the world's nations were of equal size, so that all the world's citizens were represented evenly, and even if the Security Council were abolished and no state, in the real world, was more powerful than any other, the UN would still fail the basic democratic tests, for the simple reason that its structure does not match the duties it is supposed to discharge. The United Nations has awarded itself three responsibilities. Two of these are *international* duties, namely to mediate between states with opposing interests and to restrain the way in which its members treat their own citizens. The third is a *global* responsibility: to represent the common interests of all the people of the world. But it is constitutionally established to discharge only the first of these functions.

From time to time, nearly all the UN's member states will unite to condemn a government's atrocious treatment of its citizens, such as the ethnic cleansing commissioned by the Federal Republic of Yugoslavia. But this is possible only because that country's behaviour is anomalous. There are other issues over which the interests of almost all member states are demonstrably at variance with those of their people. Defence spending is an obvious example. In most countries, from the democratic superpower to the tinpot military dictatorship, the confluence of interests which Dwight Eisenhower called 'the military-industrial complex' exercises inordinate power over government, and money which should be spent, for example, on public health and education, is instead spent on unnecessary weapons. But the member states will not unite to condemn this imposition, because almost all of them engage in it. The nation states tacitly conspire against their peoples.

For similar reasons the UN is inherently incapable of representing the common interests of all the people of the world. There is a strong argument, for example, for severely restricting the freedom of financial speculators, whose activities have in recent years wrecked several formerly healthy economies and contributed massively to the indebtedness of the poor nations. But because of the power these speculators possess to strip a nation of its financial assets, they have become the world's kingmakers. Nearly all the governments in power today are those whose policies are acceptable to the financial markets: they are, in effect, the representatives of global capital. The opposition parties who might challenge this dispensation are kept out of power partly by citizens' fear of how the markets might react if they were elected. So while it might suit the interests of nearly everyone on earth to re-impose capital controls and bring many forms of speculation to an end, the existing system suits most of the world's governments rather well, even as their populations suffer. An assembly of nation states is therefore unlikely to take the kind of collective global action which would be necessary to rid the world of this plague. The preamble to the UN Charter begins with the words 'We the peoples of the United Nations'. It would more accurately read 'We the states'.

Ever since the formation of the UN, there have been efforts to modify this undemocratic order, but few of the existing proposals address the fundamental problems. Many of them fall into one of two categories: permitting national parliamentarians to influence UN policy, and granting members of 'civil society' a consultative or, in some cases, a junior decision-making role.

The Inter-Parliamentary Union, for example, which is an association of members of national parliaments founded in 1889, now has 'consultation status' on the UN's Economic and Social Council and 'observer status' at the World Trade

Organization.[38] This permits some form of representation, albeit diffuse and indirect, for the citizens of the world. Like the e-parliament, which now provides national MPs with a virtual debating chamber,[39] the Inter-Parliamentary Union might, as some of its proponents argue, help encourage global democratization. But these initiatives also suffer from some of the constraints which limit the democratic potential of the UN General Assembly.

Every member of the Inter-Parliamentary Union or the e-parliament is subject to three conflicting pressures: the demand by her constituents that their immediate, or local, needs be met; the demand by her national party leaders that she keep to the party line; and, if they are sufficiently interested, the demand by certain of her constituents that she represent their needs or views at the global level. She will have been selected by her party largely on the grounds of her responsiveness to the second demand, and elected by her constituents largely on the grounds of her adherence to the first. These conflicting demands cause a number of problems at the international level. The first is that her main concerns are likely to be more parochial than we might wish of a truly international or global parliamentarian. Her membership of the international union, as it must take second place to her local concerns, will be something of a hobby. If ever she is faced with a conflict between the domestic needs of her constituents and their international needs, she will resolve it in favour of the former.

This is why the people of Europe are represented in the European Parliament not by their national MPs, but by special members elected for this purpose. The second problem is that she remains a member of her national party. If it discovers that her international activities conflict with its policies, it will instruct her to desist. A national party's concerns will always, of course, be overwhelmingly national.

The third problem is that as soon as the work of any international group of national MPs is taken seriously by powerful nation states, they will use the members' national interests to rein them in. This lever is repeatedly pulled by powerful states to discipline the representatives of weaker nations. When, for example, the United States wanted a UN resolution permitting it to wage war on Iraq in 1990 and discovered that some of the temporary members of the Security Council were opposed to it, it bought the votes of Zaire, Ethiopia and Colombia by persuading Saudi Arabia to offer them free oil. This helped ensure that Cuba and Yemen were the only two members of the Security Council to defy the resolution. As soon as it had been adopted, the US ambassador turned to the Yemeni representative and told him that his was 'the most expensive vote you will ever cast'.[40] Three days later, the US cancelled its $70 million of annual aid to Yemen. An international body composed of national MPs is destined either to be ineffective and ignored, or effective and crushed.

A further problem arises from the sheer number of potential representatives it mobilizes. Either all 25,000 of the world's democratically elected representatives (or however many of them can be bothered) vote on every issue, or they must surrender their powers to a committee or a subcommittee of a committee. This leads to one of two political outcomes. Either there is a gross *horizontal* diffusion of accountability, caused by the vast number of potential representatives, or there is a gross *vertical* diffusion of accountability, caused by the process of photocopy democracy.* In either case, it leaves constituents feeling that they have little real leverage over the decisions the parliament makes. Another obvious problem is that this system leaves those people who do not live in representative democracies with no opportunity to determine how the world is run. These people, perhaps more than anyone else on earth, need international or global assistance, both to undermine their oppressive governments and to secure the peace and material prosperity those governments tend to deny them. Far from offering them a means of confronting oppression, this system leaves them doubly unrepresented, placing them at a still greater global disadvantage.

---

* A horizontal diffusion means that, as decisions are split between a huge number of representatives, their individual contribution becomes so small as to be negligible, which means that they cannot individually be held to account for what happens. A vertical diffusion means that accountability becomes lost in the obscure hierarchy of committees and subcommittees.

These and other problems have encouraged some people to suggest that the democratic deficits of the United Nations should be addressed instead through the representation of 'constituencies of interest', by which they mean non-governmental organizations, or NGOs. Already, gatherings of NGOs are being granted formal rights by some international bodies. The UN's Economic and Social Council, for example, has given 'consultative status' to 1500 NGOs. In 2000, the UN hosted a 'Millennium Forum' of NGOs, whose declaration was adopted as an official UN document, and whose representative became an official delegate at the UN Summit. Several eminent scholars have called for the creation of a permanent 'NGO Forum', sitting alongside the United Nations, helping to inform and guide the decisions it makes. This would, I believe, be a disaster for democracy.

Permitting NGOs to represent the people of the earth introduces several unresolvable problems. The first is that either every body calling itself an 'NGO' must be permitted to attend, or someone must determine who can and who can't turn up.

If every self-appointed NGO is to be represented, then the diffusion of accountability which vitiates the parliamentary unions will be multiplied many times over, as every sub-faction of every possible interest group seeks to enter. If every member of an international NGO forum was to receive one vote, then we have effectively established a *plutocracy* (a political system governed by money), as the richest organizations (in particular the corporations and corporate lobby groups) could each establish several hundred separate NGOs to represent their interests. Needless to say, such a forum would be so big as to be utterly incapable of making a decision. If, on the other hand, one vote was to be allocated to each agglomeration of interest groups, we would discover, for example, that the representatives of those (few and tiny) NGOs whose members insist that the human race was sired by aliens would possess the same global power as the big development agencies. So it seems clear that someone must decide which groups can and cannot be represented. There are several possible criteria this 'someone' could apply. The most obvious is to appoint to the forum those NGOs with the biggest global membership. The world's people would then be represented by animal welfare charities and cancer research trusts.

So the Grand Inquisitor with the responsibility of deciding who qualifies would need to establish his own criteria for choosing the representatives of the people. This means that he will pre-determine the political outcome of whatever debates the NGO forum might hold. NGOs, of course, represent entrenched and generally non-negotiable interests, so simply by deciding which groups should be allowed to attend and in which proportion, the Inquisitor decides in advance how every issue will be resolved.

This is, in other words, not just an impossible task, but a ridiculous one, which leads not to the promotion of democracy but the pre-emption of democracy. And these constraints arise even before we come to consider such issues as presumed consent, accountability and the ranking of issues. The Inquisitor takes the place of the world's people in determining what is and is not important. Far from increasing the scope of popular representation, an NGO forum reduces it to the decision of one inherently unaccountable person or committee. It should not surprise the members of the global justice movement that two of our most committed enemies, the former director-general of the World Trade Organization, Michael Moore, and the European trade commissioner, Pascal Lamy, have both supported the idea of NGO representation, even though both men have questioned NGOs' transparency and accountability. It is precisely because they lack accountability that their engagement is acceptable to the dictatorship of vested interests. Whenever the NGOs it has elevated turn against it, it can, quite reasonably, dismiss them as illegitimate.

All those who live in democratic nations today would regard as intolerable a proposal to replace their national parliaments with one or other of these schemes. If a government announced that it intended to abolish parliament or congress and replace it with a union of the country's thousands of local councillors (many of whom know nothing of national politics), which would seek to legislate either as a vast and sprawling body or by means of ever more obscure subcommittees, that government should expect to be over-thrown. If it were to suggest that the task of representation should be handed instead to a forum of voluntary organizations, either self-selected or chosen by some all-powerful ombudsman, it would never recover from the ensuing ridicule.

Why such substitutes for democracy should be any more acceptable at the global level is impossible to see. If we wish to be represented, then let us be represented, and let us no longer accept the evasions, half-measures, impediments, intermediaries and arbiters whose installation masquerades as global democratization. The only genuinely representative global forum is a *directly* representative one, by which, of course, I mean a world parliament.

It is hard to think of any issue of national importance which now stops at the national frontier. The World Trade Organization has extended its mandate so far that its decisions could come to govern everything from food labelling to railway timetables. The World Bank and IMF have penetrated the poorer nations to the point at which they are, in some cases, telling their schools which brand of computers they should buy. The decisions being made by the Security Council will help to determine whether we live in peace or are perpetually subject to terrorism and war. Climate change, financial speculation, debt and deregulation reach us wherever we live. As everything has been globalized except democracy, the rulers of the world can go about their business without reference to ourselves. Unsurprisingly, therefore, many – perhaps most – of the decisions they make conflict with the interests of the majority, and reflect only those of the dominant minority.

While the rulers of the world cloister themselves behind the fences of Seattle or Genoa, or ascend into the inaccessible eyries of Doha and Kananaskis, they leave the rest of the world shut out of their deliberations. We are left to shout abuse, to hurl ourselves against the lines of police, to seek to smash the fences which stand between us and the decisions being made on our behalf. They reduce us, in other words, to the mob, and then revile the thing they have created. When, like the cardinals who have elected a new pope, they emerge, clothed in the serenity of power, to announce that it is done, our howls of execration serve only to enhance the graciousness of their detachment. They are the actors, we the audience, and for all our catcalls and imprecations, we can no more change the script to which they play than the patrons of a cinema can change the course of the film they watch. They, the tiniest and most unrepresentative of the world's minorities, assert a popular mandate they do not possess, then accuse *us* of illegitimacy. Their rule, unauthorized and untested, is sovereign.

A world parliament endows us, in theory, with three democratic resources the world does not yet possess. The first is a forum that carries weight and commands recognition, in which good ideas can do battle with bad ones. There is, of course, no guarantee that a democratically elected parliament will make sensible decisions, that people will elect those who best represent their interests or that the battles between them will always be resolved in favour of justice and distribution. But this is the risk associated with democracy everywhere. It is the risk which preserves democracy. We cannot warrant that democracy will deliver what we consider to be the right results. We can warrant that the absence of democracy will deliver the wrong ones.

The second is a system which can, in theory, hold the global and international powers to account. It gives the people of the world an opportunity to influence the decisions which affect their lives, and forces those who claim to act on our behalf to respect us.

The third is an accelerated fusion of human interests, which propels us towards the metaphysical mutation.*

By itself, the investiture of a world parliament is an insufficient measure. As part of a series of transformative actions, it is an indispensable one.

*   *   *

---

* I have used Houellebecq's term throughout this book, though it might be more accurate to describe a change in the way human beings think as an *epistemological* mutation. While metaphysics is 'the science of being', epistemology means the theory of knowledge.

While a global people's assembly has revolutionary potential, it is hardly a new idea. The first reference to the notion I have seen is contained in Alfred Tennyson's poem *Locksley Hall*, written in 1842.* Today there are at least six competing models and scores of proposals, each supported by a vocal faction. I won't try to compare them, but in seeking to choose the best version, it seems to me that a key component is simplicity.

Some of the models are staggeringly complex, demanding weighted voting, special chambers to represent minority interests, and sophisticated and elaborate means of delivering proportional representation. These are supposed to ensure that the system is as fair as it could possibly be, and in principle they could enhance a parliament's authority. But complexity undermines legitimacy. If people cannot grasp immediately how the system works, why it is relevant to them and how they can affect the decisions it makes, they will lose interest, relegating it to that evergrowing list of *things I ought to know about but have neither the time nor energy to comprehend.* Indeed, one of the impediments to public attempts to hold the dictatorship of vested interests to account is the extraordinary complexity of both the issues themselves and the structures, with their multiple layers of delegated authority, through which that dictatorship works.

---

* 'Till the war-drum throbb'd no longer, and the battle-flags were furl'd
  In the Parliament of man, the Federation of the world.'

The fewer the citizens who engage in a democratic process, the less just and less legitimate it becomes. So while we could devise an assembly which catered in advance for every possible permutation of justice, it is likely in practice to prove less just than a system without such complex safeguards. The version I've chosen is therefore the simplest of all possible models. Every adult on earth possesses one vote.

The parliament would need to be big enough to represent a wide range of views, but small enough to make decisions with efficiency. So let us say, as it permits us to deal with nice round numbers, that it should contain 600 representatives, each with a constituency of 10 million people. The implications for global justice are obvious. A resident of Ouagadougou has the same potential influence over the decisions the parliament makes as a resident of Washington. A Haitian has the same representation as a Hungarian. The people of China will possess, between them, sixteen times as many votes as the people of Germany. While, unlike other models, this design makes no special provision for the votes of the poor, their representatives will massively outnumber those of the rich. It is, in other words, a revolutionary assembly.

A further implication is that, if we are to establish 600 constituencies of even size, many of them will have to straddle national borders. This is not, as some people have suggested, a liability, but an asset. The less our representatives are bound to the demands of nationhood, the less parochial their outlook is likely to be. The more we, as constituents, are forced to share our political destiny with the people of other nations, the more we are forced to understand and engage with their concerns. Some people object that these constituencies would thereby affiliate the people of two hostile nations. So much the better. All existing constituencies lump together people with starkly different interests, crossing boundaries of wealth and poverty, farmland and industry, ethnicity and religion. If they did not, and represented, as an NGO forum does, only communities of interest, most political outcomes would be predetermined, a simple matter of arithmetic. In these circumstances, elections would be fixed by whoever established the constituency boundaries.

A key determinant of the success of a world parliament is that its members are seen to have no connection to the governments of the nations from which they come. This helps defend them from the pressures that governments might exert. If the United States told a member from Yemen that unless she changed her policies it would cut the aid it gives her country's government, she could reply that the decisions she makes have nothing to do with the government. This is not an assembly formed by nation states, but an assembly formed by the world's people. It is global, not international.

So how do we begin? We begin by liberating ourselves from the perception that we must wait upon nation states to deliver global justice. This assembly will belong to the people, and we require no one's permission to establish it. So let us picture a process which starts with a series of global meetings, open to everyone, but whose participants have not – as it has to begin somewhere – yet been elected. Let us picture, for example, the annual meetings which already engage some tens of thousands of people, organized by the World Social Forum.* These are in no sense representative assemblies. The people who attend them are self-selecting and drawn from among those who can either afford an airfare (to Brazil or India) or persuade someone else to provide one for them. But they attract citizens from most of the potential constituencies the members of a world parliament would represent.

Our first task would be to publish pamphlets and web pages explaining the idea in as many languages as we possess. Our second would be to organize a consultation of as many of the world's people, through randomly selected samples, as the budgets we raise permit, to discover whether or not our proposal commands popular consent. If the consultations reveal that the idea is unpopular, then (though we might seek to change people's minds through further publication and debate) we should cease the process of

---

* This is the biggest of the global justice movement's gatherings. In 2003, over 100,000 people took part. The first three forums have been held in Porto Alegre, in Brazil. In 2004 the meeting is likely to move to India.

development. But let us assume, for now, that most of the people we have polled approve of the proposal. We then find ourselves in a rather stronger position to raise funds, and to set up an electoral commission, staffed by professionals, with a strictly neutral mandate. This could begin to draw up boundaries and design an election. Its reports would then be disseminated for global consultation.

It is important that at this pre-democratic stage as little is decided as possible, and that all decisions made could be reversed if either public referenda or the parliament itself decided that they were wrong. The first general election, for example, could be accompanied by a full referendum on whether the parliament should, indeed, be formed, and how it should work. The process must belong to the people at every stage.

The plan then becomes more expensive, more complex and more hazardous. The first and most obvious impediment is money. A global general election is likely to cost something in the order of $5 billion,* while the establish-

---

* The data on national election costs are sparse (but for some reason more abundant for Africa than any other continent). I have taken the costs of general elections in five poor nations (Kenya, Senegal, Togo, Mozambique and Ghana) and two rich nations (the United States and Australia) and divided them by their populations to arrive at an average cost per citizen of $1.03.[41] Multiplied by the world population, this gives a very tentative $6.46 billion. I have reduced it to account for economies of scale (the election would be coordinated by a single administration).

ment of a parliament might cost around $300 million,* and its annual running costs a further $1 billion or so† (an electronic assembly would be much cheaper, but a poor substitute for a real debating chamber). A very small proportion could be raised from individuals and charitable foundations. The only bodies which possess sufficient funds to provide the rest, however, are states, the international institutions and corporations, and we should, of course, be wary of accepting money from them, for fear either that they would co-opt the assembly or that we would feel constrained to adjust our plans to their convenience. Corporate funding, for obvious reasons, should be ruled out altogether. There may be a few liberal states and perhaps even a sympathetic UN agency which would give substantial sums and expect nothing in return, and this might be deemed acceptable to both the initiators of the model and the people they consult. But

---

* The European parliament in Strasbourg, at 220,000m², cost $560 million to build.[42] If the world parliament is based in a poor nation, as I suggest later in the text, the building costs would be reduced. Construction costs an average of $567/m² in the Philippines and $657/m² in Kenya,[43] giving $124.7 million and $144.5 million respectively. I have doubled the figure and rounded it up to account for the cost of equipment and recruitment.

† The Strasbourg parliament costs $1.005 billion a year to run.[44] It is slightly bigger than the proposed world parliament (750 seats). While staff costs in a poor nation will be lower, the MPs' travel and interpretation costs will be higher, so I'm guessing that the overall expense would be roughly the same. These calculations are, of course, rudimentary. Their purpose is to provide an idea of the *order* of cost.

there is an inherent contradiction between national or international funding and the aims of a global assembly.

Some people have suggested establishing a global lottery, offering enormous prizes and attracting, as a result, plenty of punters. This, though it has some ugly implications, provides us with both independent funding and weekly publicity, as even the most hostile media would find it hard not to report the results of the 'World Parliament Draw'. An alternative is to wait for the implementation of the proposals outlined in Chapter 5, which have the potential to generate far more money than we would ever need. Even so, we can anticipate a tussle over these funds between nation states and the global assembly.

The next obvious impediment is the opposition of national governments. Democratically elected governments would be foolish to seek to impede elections to a world parliament, as they would immediately be accused of despotism. But undemocratic governments would correctly perceive such elections as subversive – their citizens are likely to acquire a taste for voting. We can anticipate, therefore, that unelected leaders would seek to prevent elections to the world parliament from taking place.

There are two possible means of defeating them. The first is to hold underground elections. These are likely to be dangerous for both the participants and the people overseeing them. They could also – as visibility is essential to democratic accountability – be captured and co-opted, possibly by the very governments which drove them underground in the first place. The other is to hold elections among the exiles of the closed constituencies. This means that the great majority of the constituents would, initially at least, be deprived of a vote, while those who lived abroad would be disproportionately powerful. But, though both solutions are far from ideal, neither should be discounted, for the very reason that they are, as the governments would fear, destabilizing. Underground elections are precisely the kind of process which could begin to coordinate and mobilize opposition to an undemocratic regime. Elections among exiles have the potential to create profound resentment within the domestic population, as it perceives that it has been deprived of choice by its government. In both cases, we employ the self-reinforcing potential of democracy. A gradient of hope is established, and nothing is so threatening to tyranny as hope. Even so, we may have to start without some regions of the world.

Building a world parliament is not the same as building a world government. We would be creating a chamber in which, if it works as it should, the people's representatives will hold debates and argue over resolutions. In the early years at least, it commands no army, no police force, no courts, no departments of government. It need be encumbered by neither president nor cabinet. But what we have created is a body which possesses something no other global or international agency can claim: legitimacy. Directly elected, owned by the people of the world, our parliament would possess the moral authority which all other bodies lack. And this alone, if effectively deployed, is a source of power.

Even those bodies whose legitimacy is at best diffuse, derivative and vague possess enough moral authority to moderate the behaviour of the world's only superpower. The government of the United States could have attacked Iraq whenever it wanted, without asking anyone's permission. It has sufficient military power to defeat any state on earth. It requires, as the president has constantly hinted, no allies to pursue its military adventures. Yet at the end of 2002, it chose to submit itself to the intensely frustrating and at times humiliating scrutiny of the other members of the United Nations Security Council. It did so because it wanted to persuade its citizens that the war it was proposing against Iraq was a just one. Opinion polls within the United States (whose people, despite the best efforts of successive governments, remain by and large civilized and humane) showed that the Americans would look more kindly upon a war which had the UN's approval. They did not want to see themselves as the citizens of a nation whose foreign policy was built entirely on brute force. The events of 2003, however, suggest that the council's limited reserves of moral power have been exhausted.

Similar concessions to moral authority constrain the behaviour of all but the most tyrannical states. The governments of the European Union have repeatedly enhanced the powers of the European Parliament, despite the fact that it competes with them for control over European decision-making.* They have done so in order to persuade their people that the Union – and therefore its governments – is democratically accountable.

Perhaps the most startling example of moral power is one which takes us back to the potential starting point for our own parliamentary assembly. The 50,000 people who gathered in Porto Alegre in Brazil for the World Social Forum in 2002 represented no one but themselves. Yet theirs was widely perceived as the only international assembly which had any claim to reflect the views of the people of the world. The result was that officials from some of the world's most powerful governments and institutions came to try to persuade the forum that they were listening. Twice as many French ministers travelled to the World Social Forum as to the World Economic Forum, the official, intergovernmental meeting which was taking place at the same time in New York.[45] Even the president of the World Bank, one of the least accountable of all international bodies, applied to speak there. But, as if to

---

* This point has been made by the legal theorists Richard Falk and Andrew Strauss.

show where moral power really lay, the forum turned him away.[46]

If even this self-selected convention can attract, without inviting them, representatives of some of the world's most powerful institutions, then we can only guess what moral power an elected global assembly might wield. A world parliament would be able to determine whether or not the international actions of a government or an institution have the support of the world's people. And as most of the world's big governments and institutions claim to act democratically, they would be drawn to our assembly like moths to a flame.

We already possess an example of a people's parliament built on moral authority, which managed to bring the world's most powerful government to heel. In the fifth century BC, Rome was governed by consuls, drawn solely from the *patrician*, or aristocratic, class. Theirs was an oppressive government, exercising absolute power over the other social classes. The record is a little hazy, but it seems that one day in 494 BC, prompted by issues which would not be unfamiliar to today's global justice movement (debt, unequal access to land and arbitrary treatment by the authorities), thousands of the *plebeians*, the working people of Rome, suddenly disappeared.[47] This event came to be known as the 'first secession of the plebs'. They had agreed to meet on the Sacred Mount, a hill outside the city. There they arranged themselves into a people's parliament – the

Consilium Plebis – and elected two *tribunes*, or representatives. All the people on the hill swore that anyone who harmed the tribunes, irrespective of class or power, would be killed.

At first the tribunes of the plebs had no constitutional powers; they could merely urge the authorities to recognize the needs of their constituents. But, backed by huge numbers, they were hard to ignore and impossible to kill. Gradually, the scope of the Consilium's powers began to increase, and in 449 BC, after a second secession of the plebs, it was officially recognized by the state. The tribunes, now ten in number, were granted a right of veto over the business of the government. The resolutions adopted by the Consilium Plebis (known as *plebiscites*) gradually began to be passed into law. The plebeians also elected a number of officials – the *aediles* – whose purpose was to record the proceedings of the Senate (the patricians' parliament), in the hope of being able to hold its members to their word, and to establish a body of written law which would protect the plebs from arbitrary treatment by magistrates.

The power of the plebs lasted for about a hundred years. By 367 BC, at least one of the tribunes had been admitted to the Senate as a consul. But (and there is surely a lesson here for all democratic movements) the transformation appears to have been rather too successful, for the tribunes began to accumulate so much power that they ceased to identify with the powerless and came, instead, to see themselves as a new ruling class. Ambitious young men began using the Tribunate as a means of entry to the Senate, and gradually the plebs' movement was taken over by the nobility. But, for a century or so, the oppressed people of Rome had moderated the power of the ruling class by means of a parliamentary assembly founded on moral authority.

There is, then, plenty of evidence to suggest that our parliament *can* work this way. But *should* it work this way? Is there an alternative to coercive power based solely on moral authority?

In the early stages at least, I don't believe there is.* The only available alternative is a parliament whose decisions are imposed on other bodies, if necessary by force of arms. This is how the Security Council works today. But the armies and the weapons it calls upon are those which reside in the hands of the state. Its coercive powers (and hence the monopoly of violence it asserts) depend on the compliance of the world's most powerful governments, which is why it is such a partisan organization. The point of a people's assembly is that it is independent of pre-existing powers. Only if the delegated officials of the parliament managed to accumulate so much weaponry that they could force every nation to do as they demanded would the parliament be able to impose its will, but that would necessitate a world

---

* I am indebted to Troy Davis for persuading me of the benefits of this approach.

government so powerful that it would swiftly become the most oppressive force on earth.

There is, moreover, a great advantage to a parliament whose power relies entirely on moral authority, and this is that it sustains this power by showing that it continues to command the support of the people. If it loses touch with the people, it loses much of its force. This has the potential, then, to be a self-regulating system.

So we are left with an assembly whose primary purpose is to hold other powers to account. It would review the international decisions made by governments, by the big financial institutions, and by bodies such as the United Nations and the World Trade Organization. Through consultation with the world's people and through debates within the chamber, it would establish the broad principles by which these other bodies should be run. It would study the decisions they make and hold them up to the light. When it discovers that they have breached the principles of good governance it has established, it would pass resolutions and publish critical reports. We have every reason to believe that, if properly constituted, our parliament, as the only body with a claim to represent the people of the world, would force them to respond.

Let us picture a situation, for example, in which a body such as the World Bank had decided to pay for the construction of a giant hydro-electric dam. The villagers whose homes were due to be flooded might approach the world parliament and ask it to examine the bank's decision. The parliament would ask the bank for its comments, and perhaps send a fact-finding mission to the site of the dam. It would then judge the scheme by the principles it had established. If it found that the dam fell short of those principles, it would say so. The bank could refuse either to change the project or to withdraw its funding, but only if it was prepared to lose credibility. Judging by the success of an unelected and little-known body called the World Commission on Dams in forcing the World Bank to promise to change the way it operates,* I think we can expect the bank to consider itself obliged to respond to the world parliament's decisions.

The same approach could be used, though to a lesser extent, to change some of the underlying principles governing the way the big international bodies operate. If our parliament, for example, ruled that the World Trade Organization's decisions are unfair because they are made by committees of corporate lawyers meeting in secret, I think we could expect the WTO to change those procedures. But it would soon collide with some intractable political realities. We could not expect our assembly to be able to prevent

---

* The World Bank has since been accused of backtracking,[48] but the WCD's report has proved invaluable to the people seeking to hold it to account.

dictators from murdering their people or powerful states from invading other nations. The parliament might decide that the IMF, the World Bank and the WTO should dissolve themselves, but without any expectation that they would feel prompted to do so. Such tasks will require a different approach, which I will explain in subsequent chapters. The world parliament is the body which could hold our new, more responsive institutions to account.

But we can see how the power of this parliament could be enhanced even by those agencies which would rather it did not exist. Once citizens came to the parliament with a complaint, the bodies they were criticizing would feel obliged to respond. By responding, they would validate and recognize the parliament's authority. By recognizing its authority once, their obligation to respond on the following occasion would increase: they would gradually find themselves handing more power to the parliament. In this respect, as in many others, democracy can be self-establishing.

While the main function of our parliament, in the early years at least, may be to hold other bodies to account, it is also possible to see how it could begin to propose and initiate measures of its own. Though we cannot anticipate the novel solutions to some of the world's problems which an assembly, freely guided by its electors, might devise, it is not hard to see how the parliament might help to promote some of the progressive measures which have already been projected but have so far proved impossible to implement.

The only just and sustainable means of tackling climate change, for example, is 'contraction and convergence', the model designed by the concert viola player and obsessively effective campaigner Aubrey Meyer.[49] This scheme first establishes how much carbon dioxide and other greenhouse gases humans can produce each year without frying the planet. It then divides that sum between all the people of the world, and allocates to each nation, on the basis of its population, a quota for gas production. It proposes a steady reduction (or 'contraction') of both the total world production of climate-changing gases and the excessive production within nations which currently exceed their quotas. National production per head of population gradually 'converges' to equality; any nation which wants to produce more than its share must first buy unused quota from another one.

The model has been approved by ministers and government scientists in dozens of countries, and now appears to be the favoured solution of the United Nations and even the World Bank. But, because it conflicts with their national interests, none of the governments which claim to support it appear prepared to implement it, or even to champion it with any vigour. While we don't know how a world parliament might respond to this idea, it is easy to see why, if it did adopt the model as policy, it could prove to be a far more effective advocate than either governments or the existing international bodies, all of which are constrained by national politics. It might also become a powerful defender of multilateral disarmament, a global tax (the 'Tobin tax') on financial speculation, or the UN's proposal that the rich nations should each devote 0.7 per cent of their national wealth to foreign aid.

In every case, if the parliament agreed that these were worthy goals, it could play the role of honest broker: an agency unconstrained by competition between nations. Indeed, we may well find that national governments begin to turn to the parliament for the arbitration of political matters, much as they use the International Court of Justice for the settlement of legal disputes today. In doing so, they would, of course, be recognizing and reinforcing the parliament's moral authority.

This, at any rate, is how we might expect our assembly to begin. But democracy demands that we make no attempt to prescribe how it should evolve. It may continue to exercise such modest functions as I have already described. It may, if the people will it and if states begin formally to recognize its powers, become a legislative body. This could begin to establish a body of global law supported – uniquely – by democratic consent. While the parliament would continue to exert no direct control over nation states, those which have signed a treaty granting it certain formal powers are likely to feel bound by the laws it passes, or risk the loss of credibility. It could become the legislature which

THE AGE OF CONSENT

complements and helps legitimate the judicial authority of the International Criminal Court.* Or, if the people of the world demand this, it could begin to establish the rudiments of a global government, accumulating certain powers hitherto vested only in the hands of nation states. But it is not for those of us who propose this body to make such decisions. The point of democracy is that it gets out of control; no person or faction, least of all those who design the system which starts the process, should be able to steer it. The parliament must come to belong to the world's people, not to the authors of the model.

If you respond with horror to the idea of a world parliament, as many do, I would invite you to examine your reaction carefully. Is it because you believe that such a body might become remote and excessively powerful? Or is it really because you cannot bear the idea that a resident of Brussels would have no greater voice in world affairs than a resident of Kinshasa? That the Ethiopians would elect the same number of representatives as the Italians (and more as their

---

* The ratification of the ICC, in 2002, could be viewed as the first clear victory for democratic globalization. It is in some respects a *global* criminal court as, unlike the International Court of Justice, its resolutions do not depend on direct brokerage between nation states. It came into being partly as a result of determined lobbying by civil society, in particular the Coalition for the International Criminal Court, which is a network of over 1000 NGOs.

population increases)? That the people of Mexico would, collectively, become two and a half times as powerful as the people of Spain, while the Indians would cast seventeen times as many votes as the inhabitants of the United Kingdom? That, in other words, the flow of power established when a few nations ruled the world would be reversed? Are you afraid that this parliament might threaten democracy, or are you really afraid that it would actuate it?

In the heart of even the most radical European or North American campaigner lurks, I suspect, a residual fear of the Yellow Peril, of the people of other lands, who do not share our worldview, becoming too powerful. We might lament the excessive power of the United Nations Security Council, but are we not, in some secret recess of the heart, also thankful that our governments can force the world to comply with their demands? Which of us in the rich world is not aware that we have benefited, through public spending, safe housing and secure food supplies, from the power our government wields over others? Which of us does not offer a secret prayer of thanks to the earthly powers who have decreed that we need entertain no fear of invasion? Which of us, in other words, cannot see that the current dispensation of power relieves us of the need to break the economic grip of our own ruling classes, which, without the fruits of the colonial economy, would be so oppressive as to compromise our prospects of survival? Which of us cannot see that our government's power to demand the compliance of other nations permits us to be complacent about the treatment of those nations, knowing as we do that they cannot punish our violations with conquest? Which of us, at heart, is not an oligarch?

If, as we claim, we belong to a 'global justice movement', then we must be prepared to accept the loss of our own nations' power to ensure that the world is run for our benefit. In rising against the excessive powers of our governments, we must rise against our own instincts: against the fear of other people's freedom, against the indolence which recognizes that our freedom not to act relies on their incapacity to act. Unless we are prepared to take our arguments to their logical conclusion, we may as well furl our banners and go home.

Few people frankly admit that they fear the freedom of the people of other nations; but when they do, they tend to argue that this freedom would compromise our own. Joseph Nye, for example, dean of the Kennedy School of Government at Harvard University, is one of the fiercest opponents of a world parliament. It would permit, he claims, the 'citizens of around 200 states' (the rest of the world) to 'be continually outvoted by more than a billion Chinese and a billion Indians'. The result would be 'a nightmare' for those who 'seek to promote international environmental and labor standards, as well as democracy'.[50]

This assertion appears to rely on several curious assumptions. The first is that the Chinese or the Indians would vote not according to what they wanted, but according to their nationality. The second is that the people of these nations would vote against the people of the rest of the world. He fails to explain why the interests of people in China or India should be at variance with those of everyone else. We could surely expect the impoverished textile workers of China, India, Bangladesh, Mexico and Haiti to express quite similar interests. We can further expect their choices to be at variance with those of their employers, which are likely to be more consonant with those of the Western elite.

Professor Nye further assumes, again without explanation, that the people of China and India would vote against higher environmental and labour standards, and even against democracy. Why the people of the biggest democracy on earth would seek to overturn democracy is not clear. As several revolutions and attempted revolutions, a successful decolonization movement and the extraordinary courage of those who stood against the tanks in Tiananmen Square suggest, the people of China and India are just as capable of assessing their political options and making rational decisions as anyone else. Nor is it obvious that the people who suffer most from low environmental and labour standards would be the keenest to keep them that way. Indeed, the world's biggest environmental movements are in India, and in both nations there is constant agitation, though often brutally suppressed in China, for higher labour standards. While the bosses of Chinese and

Indian corporations might vote to keep their employees in a state of near-slavery, we would, I think, have good reason to assume that their workers would not vote the same way.

The truth is that many people in the West, as they have done for centuries, entertain a lively hatred of the Chinese. We have long chosen to see them as faceless masses, statistics rather than human beings, without the capacity for reason or freewill, who prefer to be told what to do than to make their own decisions. One hundred and fifty years ago, we hated them for refusing to trade with us and for rebelling against our economic impositions. Now we appear to hate them for trading too successfully, and because we fear they *won't* rebel against our economic impositions. In both cases, our hatred reflects our unvoiced fear that they might become free and in doing so challenge the unjust world order which permits us to oppress them. Of course, we cannot guarantee that the people of India and China will always vote for democracy and for higher environmental and labour standards – the point of democracy is that you cannot guarantee anything. But we can be sure that the current system of global governance will continue to discriminate *against* these advancements.

Conversely, others have maintained that a global parliament would be yet another imposition of Western political and cultural values upon the rest of the world. This argument is also founded on a presumption that democracy is alien to the people of non-Western nations. In truth, the majority of those who live in parliamentary democracies, flawed as some of them may be, live in the poor world. Those of us who have worked in such nations can attest that few of their inhabitants would prefer to be governed by a different system. It is true to say that the model on which many of their parliaments are based was first developed in the West, but it is also the case that this model no longer belongs exclusively to the West.

We can hope and expect, moreover, that as our parliament belongs to the people from the beginning of the process, it would differ from, and be an improvement on, the kind of democracy which prevails in the rich world. Guided by the consent of the electors, it should evolve its own political dynamic, which reflects the combined will of all the world's people and, because of the weight of numbers, particularly those who do not live in the Western nations. But our greatest safeguard against imposition is to ensure that nothing is imposed; if, in the initial referenda, the people of the world reject a world parliament, then a world parliament will not come into existence.

These concerns do, however, suggest the need for a further safeguard in the form of a new referendum every ten or twenty years, which would permit the people of the world to vote for the parliament's dissolution. This would be particularly important if we had to begin without some regions of the world, because of the opposition of their governments. It would help to protect the world not only against the imposition of the values of a minority, but also against the possibility that our parliament may itself accumulate oppressive powers.

A variant on this objection is that the creation of a world parliament depends on a sense of global nationhood which does not yet exist. Joseph Nye argues that 'there is little evidence that a sufficiently strong sense of community exists at the global level' on which we could build a parliament. The world would first require 'a widespread sense of identity as a citizenry as a whole'.[51]

It is surely clear that parliamentary democracy does not depend on a strong sense of community. Within even the longest-established democratic states there are large numbers of distinct communities, which share little sense of engagement with their neighbours other than the fact that they inhabit the same nation and vote in the same elections. Professor Nye's own country, the United States of America, offers, perhaps, the definitive example of diversity co-existing with democracy. The ultra-conservative Christian communities of the deep South, for example, could scarcely have less in common with the gay and hippy communities of San Francisco. The poor Hispanic districts of Los Angeles are a world apart from the mansions of Beverly Hills. The nation's Orthodox Jews and fundamentalist Muslims could scarcely be said to see themselves as comrades. Yet no one in the US argues that democracy there is impossible because an 'insufficiently strong sense of community exists at the national level'.

Indeed, all nationhood is to some extent artificial, the product of historical accident, the convenience of tyrants and the disengagement of colonists. It is hard to think of any nation whose members belong to just one religious, ethnic or tribal community. Even the tiny Pacific island states incorporate tribes which once collected each other's heads as trophies. Nations do not fall apart at every general election just because their people think in different ways; in fact most communities unconsciously reinforce the democratic process by vying to make that process work for themselves. The expansion of the European Union requires that the Hungarians must now perceive that they have a common destiny with the Portuguese, but not – at least until 2007 – with the Romanians. The Greeks must reconcile themselves to the idea that they may, one day, belong to the same community of nations as the Turks, but might never belong to the same confederation as the Russians. If we believe that this political project is viable, and that the people of the European Union are sufficiently adaptable and far-sighted to accept these staggeringly arbitrary distinctions, then we should surely have no difficulty in seeing the potential viability of a global political identity.

The world's population, by contrast to those of its nation states, is a self-defined entity, a country whose borders are indisputable, whose sense of common destiny requires no patriotic speeches, no hanging of flags, no wars with other worlds. Though most of us have yet to acknowledge it, a global identity – rather, a species identity – has been there from the moment our ancestors first walked upon two legs. The demagogues who have created nations and established empires have sought to justify their governance by suggesting that the people who live beyond their borders are fundamentally different from those within. But now that the racial stereotyping required by empire is beginning to abate (or rather, because of the multi-ethnic character of the powerful nations, to be reserved only for the *leaders* of the enemy), many humans are coming to see that the other members of the species have broadly the same needs and responses, and that these needs and responses differ in some respects from those of other species. The nationhood of human beings, what Alfred Tennyson called the Parliament of Man, is pre-established.

Indeed, by making this political identity visible, by creating a forum in which the people of diverse nations can unite on some issues and divide on others, irrespective of nationhood, our parliament has the potential to begin to establish a sense of common destiny, to start the process of catalysis which foments the metaphysical mutation.

But here we do encounter a real conflict, though for precisely the opposite reasons to those advanced by the good professor. Is there not a clash between the universalism of human concerns and the diversity of human cultures?

Could our world parliament, and the other measures proposed here – or, for that matter, the metaphysical mutation itself – not accelerate the destruction of the distinct forms of social organization which so many of us in the global justice movement rightly wish to defend? This is not the fey or aesthetic concern that some universalists have suggested. The diversity of human cultures is valuable not only because it makes the world a fascinating place. Many cultures have evolved the subtlest of responses, honed over hundreds of generations, to environmental constraints. The anthropologist Darrell Posey has shown, for example, how the Kayapó of the southern Amazon have developed a farming system which permits them to survive in places otherwise hostile to agriculture.[52] They cultivate fire-resistant sweet potatoes, which catch the nutrients released when tree-trunks are burnt, and a staple crop which both produces its own pesticides, and, through a commensal relationship with a species of ant, weeds itself. Their survival relies on a refined appreciation of microclimates and the relationships between animals and plants. By contrast to almost all the more recently established cultivators in the Amazon, they both improve the soil, and, through planting islands of useful trees in the savannah, expand the forest cover.

Their techniques are encoded in their songs and stories, and in concepts which cannot be successfully translated into other languages. Their language and their sense of self-worth, like those of most of the world's indigenous people, are now threatened; in this case by a combination of economic globalization, political oppression and the seizure of their resources by other Brazilians. This compromises not only their own economic survival, but also the survival of the ecosystems in which they live. Nor are indigenous people the tiny minority we often imagine. According to the United Nations, they comprise some five per cent of the world's population, or 300 million souls.

There is a conflict here that cannot be denied. There has always been a struggle between diversity and universalism. Those who, like most of the members of the global justice movement, wish to promote universal human rights find themselves at odds with cultural distinction whenever they contest female genital mutilation or the stoning of adulterers. By bringing people together politically, we are likely to enhance the use of common languages and common ways of thinking. We might also discover that we accelerate economic globalization. All these factors have the potential further to undermine cultural identity.

But we also invoke a countervailing force, in the form of an unparalleled opportunity for advocacy. Already, indigenous representatives are making better use of international bodies than any other citizens' groups, except, perhaps, development NGOs. Every few months, there are assemblies of people from all over the world whose cultures are threatened. Inuits from Greenland find common cause with the Dani of West Papua; the Maya agree strategy with the Maori. It is arguable that all that prevents the final destruction of most of the world's indigenous peoples is the support which they and their defenders can summon from beyond their own national borders. By appealing to universalism, they defend diversity.

A world parliament provides indigenous people with more potent opportunities for mobilizing global support. A parliamentary resolution condemning the treatment of the Saami in Norway or the Aborigines in Australia could, for example, be profoundly embarrassing to the democratically elected governments of those countries. At present, the coercive power of economic globalization is unmatched by the moral power of political globalization. One paradoxical outcome of the Age of Consent could be that we cultivate a universal consciousness of the right to be different.

But these considerations do convey a warning for our democratic model: that we should be wary of striving for perfection. We must accept that democracy will always be something of a mess. Attempting to tidy it up too much could mean subordinating diversity to universalism and the individual consciousness to the general will to such an extent that we may establish the preconditions not for freedom but for captivity. We must leave gaps between the building blocks, in case we accidentally build a wall.

Indeed, there is no clearer exposition of the dangers of excessive tidiness than one of the most advanced and most visible plans for a world parliament, the scheme presented by a gathering of academics, bureaucrats and other worthy people who call themselves the World Constitution and Parliament Association.[53] The Association's proposals have carefully eliminated all the uncertainties introduced by global democracy, by pre-ordaining its outcomes.

Without consultation or election, it has drawn up a 'Constitution for the Federation of Earth'. This provides for a world parliament consisting of three chambers, namely an elected 'House of Peoples', an appointed 'House of Nations', and a 'House of Counsellors', whose purpose is 'to represent the highest good and best interests of humanity as a whole'.[54] Members of the House of Counsellors will be proposed by representatives of the world's universities, colleges and scientific institutions, otherwise identifiable as 'people like us'. These guardians of 'the highest good' will kindly spare the rest of us the trouble of choosing a World President. The parliament will be accompanied by a 'World Administration', consisting of thirty departments of government, whose duties and powers have already been determined by the Association. It will possess a 'Presidium', an 'Integrative Complex', a 'World Ombudsmus', an 'Office of World Attorneys General', a 'World Supreme Court' and any number of other grand posts and positions, some of which already appear to have been filled. Its decisions will be 'enforced' by the 'World Police' which, 'armed only with weapons appropriate for the apprehension of the individuals responsible for violation of world law', will perform such light duties as ridding the world of nuclear weapons. Happily, they won't encounter much resistance, as 'all member nations shall disarm as a condition for joining and benefiting from the world federation, subject to Article X VII, Sec. C-8 and D-6' of the World Constitution.

The Association has also been so good as to devise, in advance, the laws which will govern us. They have composed a 'Bill of Rights', in eighteen sections, a set of 'Directional Principles', in nineteen sections, and a 'Jurisdiction of World Government' which is 'defined in Grant of Powers of forty sections'.[35] Just in case the world's people might be tempted, despite such foresight on the part of our guardian-philosophers, to alter these arrangements, the evolution of the world government has already been ordained, in 'first', 'second' and 'operative' stages. In short, world democracy has been planned so conscientiously that nothing has been left to chance, least of all that frightening and uncontrollable phenomenon called choice.

If democracy is not self-establishing, it is not democracy. Any system we initiate must contain the scope for its own transformation or improvement, for all the unanticipated developments propelled by the collective genius of free debate. Far from seeking to pre-ordain its outcomes, we must pre-ordain only the openness required to permit its electors' chosen outcomes to evolve.

Some critics might suggest that we need to prescribe 'subsidiarity', the principle that decision-making will always be devolved to the lowest possible level. But while we would do well to hope that our assembly does not become so intrusive or so pettifogging as to seek to wrench control of national or local policy from national and local parliaments, there are three problems with seeking to restrict its scope in advance. The first is that it is unnecessary: while states continue to exist, they will, or so we should expect, contest its ability to reach far into their domestic politics.* The second is that the line between what is properly the preserve of a national government or a global body can be established only by practice, rather than principle: it is hard to prescribe, for example, the extent to which a government's sovereignty should be challenged when it treats its own people without humanity; the answer is likely to be different in every case. The third is that we should not seek to pre-empt the will of future generations. Faced with conditions yet more extreme than those to which we are responding today, they might, for example, decide that the nation state retains no relevance or purpose. Though we should be wary of parliamentarians seeking to seize too many powers for themselves at the expense of their constituents, their scope for abuse should be curtailed by our refer-

---

* The European Union has intruded so far into domestic policy because it was initially an international body, empowered to do so by the member states.

endum, every ten or twenty years, on whether or not the parliament should be dissolved.

Some members of the global justice movement have argued that even the most open parliamentary model limits the scope of democratic choice, for the simple reason that it relies on representation rather than participation. There is no question that representative democracy is a clumsy system. The model proposed here permits people to represent 'us' even if they were fiercely opposed by forty-nine per cent of their constituents. We elect them once, yet they continue to represent us throughout their term of office, even if we later change our minds. We may vote for them because we agree either with the policies they choose to emphasize or with the majority of the policies they propose, or simply because their policies are not as bad as those of the other candidates. But once in office, they may press for other policies which very few of their constituents would support.

But, while representation without participation is clumsy, participation without representation is simply the dictatorship of those who turn up. The participants in any global gathering must be – by comparison with most of the world's people – rich, for they can afford to travel and to take time off from work. They must possess passports and enjoy freedom of movement, which means that participation is also the privilege of people who are both permitted to leave their home states and to enter the state in which the meeting is being held, without being turned away as suspected refugees. Similar constraints govern electronic direct democracy: only the rich or the educated have access to the necessary technology, and only the free are permitted to use it.

The truth is that 'direct democracy' of this kind is, at the global level at least, a form of representative democracy, but one in which the participants appoint themselves to represent the views of the rest of the world, rather than being elected. Like the academics and bureaucrats who run the World Constitution and Parliament Association, they would be seizing, without a popular mandate, the power to determine how the world should be run.

But there is no reason why our representative system cannot be tempered with some forms of participation. We could envisage, for example, public consultations on major decisions, especially those with constitutional significance. There also seems to be a strong case for constituency ballots. If, for example, the members of a constituency managed to gather a certain number of signatures for a petition, they could demand a referendum on a decision their representative was about to make. Perhaps we could also introduce the possibility of a constituency vote of no confidence in its representative. If successful, this would force a by-election: a possibility guaranteed to concentrate the mind of any parliamentarian beginning to pull away from her electorate.

*   *   *

These safeguards alone might prove inadequate for the defence of the world parliament against all the undemocratic pressures likely to confront it. Any body which becomes politically effective will attract the attention of groups – some of which will be extremely well-resourced and adept at persuasion – hoping to obtain special favours. Democracy everywhere is compromised by the lobbying power of special interest groups, particularly those representing the interests of large corporations and powerful religious groups. Those of us who have studied the co-option of democracy in nation states or at the European level are familiar with a range of well trodden techniques. The richest lobby groups will establish offices with a permanent staff large enough to outclass any competing interest, assign intelligent and well-rewarded people to work on a particular issue, and gradually wear down the resistance of our elected representatives.

In many nations, their assaults on democracy have been helped by their financial contributions to political candidates or parties. They may also resort to criminal bribery or, as I have documented elsewhere,[56] to subtle or less subtle forms of blackmail. The candidates themselves, if they are either extremely rich or have the backing of someone who is, can effectively buy votes through blanket advertising, handing out presents, or paying for some grandiose and visible gift to the public, such as a free party, street lights, even a football stadium, just before the election takes place.

All these distortions are compounded, on a daily basis, by the media organizations controlled by another special interest group (which is often affiliated to the powerful corporate or religious groups): the multi-millionaires who own them. Max Hastings, formerly editor of the British newspaper the *Daily Telegraph*, afforded his readers a rare exposure of proprietorial pressure, when writing about his boss, Conrad Black.[57]

> Like most tycoons, Conrad was seldom unconscious of his responsibilities as a member of the rich men's trade union. Those who have built large fortunes seldom lose their nervousness that some ill-wisher will find means to take their money away from them. They feel an instinctive sympathy for fellow multi-millionaires, however their fortunes have been achieved ... Not infrequently, adverse comment in our newspaper about some fellow mogul provoked Conrad's wrath. Our excellent art critic, Richard Dorment, once wrote scathingly about the malign influence on the international art market of the vastly rich Walter Annenberg ... It took some days of patient argument to dissuade Conrad from insisting upon Dorment's execution for speaking unkindly of his old friend Walter.[58]

By appointing editors who represent and anticipate their points of view and by instilling the fear of 'execution' into their employees, proprietors ensure that their opinions dominate and therefore distort the way their newspapers, television and radio channels and websites report everything from government initiatives and popular demonstrations to, as we have seen, the structure of the art market. Almost all multi-millionaires are fiercely opposed to the furtherance of the interests of the poor, as they have, by definition, benefited from inequality. Even those with rather subtler politics than Conrad Black's are encouraged to advance the interests of capital by the requirements of their advertisers, who do not wish to discover a promotion of their new car on one page, and an article about the adverse impact of private transport on the next. The great majority of the world's media helps to limit our political choices by misrepresenting them.

There are no definitive solutions to the distorting influence of lobbyists and multi-millionaires, as it is in the nature of all special interest groups that they will find enterprising means of negotiating the barriers we might raise against them. But there are plenty of lessons to be learnt from systems which possess insufficient safeguards. We should, for example, consider introducing a strict limit on the amount of money that any candidate or party can spend on seeking election. There is also a case for restricting the size of individual donations to the equivalent of a few tens of dollars, if individual donations are to be permitted at all. Some nations are beginning to discover that the only fair system for funding candidates is state sponsorship. Our parliament, of course, has no state to draw on, but one of the other proposals presented in this book would generate many tens of billions of dollars, some of which we could hope to secure for the perpetuation of our parliament and the funding of its candidates. Even so, we would need to lay down rules governing the sources of money both the parliament and the parliamentarians are permitted to use, and preventing any of its possible sponsors (nation states or other institutions) from influencing the decisions it makes. It seems to me that it would be better to run a skeleton parliament which can discharge only a few of the functions we might envisage than a lavishly funded one which belongs to its sponsors.

It is hard to see how we might prohibit the inordinate activities of the professional lobbyists without also prohibiting the petitions, complaints and suggestions from the public (and the counter-petitions from the institutions about which the public might complain) whose consideration is a large part of the business of a responsive global parliament; but we might be able to prevent our representatives from being unduly influenced by the special interest groups. One defence is full freedom of information. If parliamentarians are acting in our interests, then they should have nothing to hide from us. We have every reason to be suspicious of public servants who refuse to let us see what they are doing.

Our global representatives would not be able to argue that they are prevented from disclosing full details of all the meetings and discussions they attend by concerns about 'national security', as they would have no national security interests to defend. Our world parliament can therefore be more transparent than any national parliament. In combination with our proposed ability to sack our representatives, either individually or en masse, this provision is likely to give us plenty of scope for forcing them out of the arms of the powerful. We might also establish a strict definition of corruption, and call upon the International Criminal Court to help us prosecute any representative who breaks the rules.

Of course the constraint which then emerges is the reporting of our representatives' activities, and of the circumstances governing the decisions they make. Those who rely for their information on the mass media, owned by multi-millionaires, are unlikely to discover that their representatives have been too responsive to multi-millionaires. They may also be gravely misled about the global context in which a debate is taking place, and the implications of the possible decisions the parliament might make. A mass media which systematically distorts our perception of the way the world is run is one of the greatest impediments to democratic choice. There is no easy solution to this problem. Any attempt to lay down rules governing the way the world's affairs are reported would be either unenforceable or oppressive. The gravest distortions, for example, often arise from the media's omissions: by ignoring the outrages commissioned by the powerful but emphasizing those perpetrated by the weak, and by disregarding the needs of the oppressed while championing those of the oppressor, their factually correct but partial reports can be just as misleading as their misreporting. It is not clear how one might legislate to prevent this. And if legislation was so prescriptive that it could govern editorial choice, it would surely also be so prescriptive as to curtail the freedom of speech which is one of the predeterminants of democracy.

The best we can do, I believe, is to seek to establish competing sources of information. Already the global justice movement has produced thousands of websites, magazines, videos, pamphlets and books. Most of them reach only those who are interested already, and our resources are limited by comparison to those of the corporations with which we are competing. But their audience appears to be growing. The role of the world's alternative media is rather like that of the *aediles*, the parliamentary reporters appointed by the *Consilium Plebis*. As our movement grows, the ratio of *aediles* to other citizens will increase accordingly, until, perhaps, we can begin to tip the balance against the mainstream media.

One of our great challenges is to reach people who are illiterate and without access to technology. This task requires hundreds of thousands of volunteers: it responds, in other words, to our strengths. There are plenty of well-developed techniques, perhaps the most effective being those devised by the Brazilian educationalist Paulo Freire, for both raising people's awareness of the underlying causes of the problems they confront, and assisting them to listen sceptically to the voices of the powerful.[59] Interestingly, we may be helped here by national governments, which in a desperate attempt to reawaken people's interest in politics (and thus enhance their democratic legitimacy) have introduced citizenship lessons to schools. These, in some countries, draw upon the liberal and liberating techniques of the barefoot pedagogists.

There are a few other measures which could help to ensure that our parliamentarians continue to represent their constituents rather than just the most aggressive special interest groups. The first is to defend them from their own party structures. In most of the world's parliaments, representatives are controlled by their party managers. On those issues considered by their leaders to be important, they are told how to vote. Indeed, a 'free vote' in some systems is seen as a luxury, to be exercised only when the party leadership either wishes to prevent a parliamentary rebellion or regards the issue as so inconsequential that it does not matter which way the decision goes. Parliamentarians, moreover, are expected, in their speeches and public statements, to place their loyalty to the party and its policies above their other concerns. These restraints, often described as the 'whipping system', can be enforced with ferocity. Members of parliament in Britain, for example, have complained of discovering that ballot papers have been completed for them in advance, of being assaulted in the corridors of the House of Commons by the 'Whips', and of being warned that if they do not do as the party says, embarrassing details of their private lives will be passed to the tabloid newspapers.[60] British MPs know that they have no chance of promotion unless they do precisely as they are told.

The whipping system, in other words, is a system of blackmail. Its purpose is to prevent our representatives from discharging their democratic duty, namely to vote and act according to their consciences, informed by the interests of their constituents. That this system supplants our control of our representatives with control by the party hierarchy; that it ensures that party leaders rather than constituents are represented in the decisions they make; and that the interests of the leadership are often at variance with the interests of constituents, is so obvious that we surely tolerate this system only because it is familiar to us.

Leaders of the governing party often maintain that this system is the only means of implementing their political programmes. They promised in their manifestos to introduce a body of legislation, and they can complete that programme only if parliamentarians do as they are told. But hardly anyone votes for everything in a party's manifesto, and most voters for most parties are unhappy with at least a few of the manifesto's promises. These promises, moreover, while so sacred when they prove to be politically expedient, turn out to be disposable as soon as a government encounters more opposition from vested interests than it expected.

We should surely expect our representatives both to be able to force the governing party to review the promises with which their constituents are unhappy, and to keep the promises for which their constituents voted.

Of course, if in the initial stages our world parliament has no executive and no direct legislative mandate, this excuse is removed outright. But in all parliamentary systems, democratic consent, if it is to mean anything at all, surely requires that party officials are forbidden to seek to interfere with the decisions our representatives make. In our world parliament, we might add this provision to those rules on corruption which could be enforced with the help of the International Criminal Court.

A further protection could be to keep the salaries of the parliamentarians relatively low. In countries in which the parliamentary wage is much greater than the national average wage, the representatives are removed from the people. Their salary encourages them to see themselves as a ruling class.

Those who defend high wages for representatives argue that they are necessary to attract the 'best' candidates, and that they protect the successful candidates from corruption, as they do not need to supplement their wages. But it seems to me that the 'best' candidates are the men and women who are prepared to subordinate their own interests to those of the people they are supposed to represent. High wages attract greedy people. If MPs are paid less, then people who are interested only in self-advancement are likely to keep away from parliament. Instead of lamenting their disappearance, as most of those in the political classes do, we should wish them good riddance.

In the early 1990s, Brazil's congressmen sought to eliminate corruption (or this, at any rate, was their excuse) by awarding themselves the highest parliamentary salaries in the world. All that happened was that they gained sufficient legitimate wealth to hide the extra money some of them made by taking bribes. No one could now point to their new cars and new houses as proof that they were taking money to which they were not entitled. High wages, moreover, as anyone who has studied remuneration in the corporate sector knows, appear not to satisfy greed, but to encourage it.

There seems to be an argument, then, for pegging global parliamentary salaries somewhere close to the global average wage. There is also a case for preventing our representatives from taking money from any other source during their term in office – representing us should be a full-time job. These are all high, even draconian, standards to demand of our representatives, but the paradox of parliament is that the more their options are restrained, the more open our system remains.

For similar reasons, we might demand that the parliament should be established in a poor country. While this may permit parliamentarians to see themselves as superior to those who live around them, that hazard is likely to be counteracted by their absorption of the perspectives of those they encounter while on parliamentary business. If we wish to contest the excessive power of the wealthiest nations, we harm our cause by permitting our assembly to be based in one of them.

Counter-democratic pressures of the kind I have listed here are often advanced as arguments against a world parliament. If we have so much difficulty holding our national representatives to account, would that difficulty not be compounded at the global level? It is certainly true that the greater the scale on which an organization operates, the less responsive it tends to become to the people it is supposed to serve. It is also true that it is harder to coordinate the opposition of ten million people to a policy, especially if they are distributed across national borders, than the opposition of ten thousand people. But all the counter-democratic pressures listed here operate whether a world parliament exists or not. Indeed, they are far more potent when applied to bodies which have no claim to democratic legitimacy, by which I mean all the current organs of global governance. Abandoning the idea of a world parliament does not mean that these pressures go away, simply that we have no means of preventing them from being exerted. The alternative to a world parliament, in other words, is not *no* global governance, but governance by a few self-appointed and unaccountable men in the rich world. That democracy is hazardous and uncertain of success is not an argument against democracy. It is an argument for public vigilance.

But a world parliament will rapidly discover that there are limits to its powers. Its moral authority will force international bodies to amend some of their practices; it will not, as I have suggested, persuade them to close themselves down. Nor, without resort to armed force, will it be able to prevent conflict between states or prevent a state from murdering its people. While nation states exist, political globalization, however legitimate, must be accompanied by internationalism, if we are to retain any possibility of preventing international violence. This suggests that if there is to be a corrective to global governance by means of brute force, we will continue to require an international body which attempts to broker peace between armed states. We could (and should) disinvent the United Nations Security Council, but we would swiftly discover that we had to develop another organization, with a similar mandate.

If such a body is to be regarded as both legitimate and authoritative, it must surely be seen to operate by means of consent, rather than coercion. This suggests that the organization responsible for global security should be as democratic as an *international* body can be.

A democratic security system would be controlled not by five self-appointed governments, but by the entire General

Assembly. Each nation's vote would be weighted according to both the number of people it represents and the democratic legitimacy it possesses.

The government of Tuvalu, representing 10,000 people, would, then, have a far smaller vote than the government of China. But China, in turn, would possess far fewer votes than it would if its government was democratically elected. Rigorous means of measuring democratization are beginning to be developed by bodies such as the Centre for Business and Policy Studies in Sweden and Democratic Audit in the United Kingdom. It would not be hard, using their criteria, to compile an objective global index of democracy. Governments, under this system, would be presented with a powerful incentive to democratize: the more democratic they became, the greater would be their influence over world affairs.

No nation would possess a veto. The most consequential decisions – to go to war for example – should require an overwhelming majority of the assembly's weighted votes. This means that powerful governments wishing to recruit reluctant nations to their cause would be forced to bribe or blackmail most of the rest of the world to obtain the results they wanted. The nations whose votes they needed most would be the ones whose votes were hardest to buy.

This body and the world parliament are likely both to enhance each other's legitimacy and to restrain each other's actions. The incentive to democratize would discourage governments from banning elections to a world parliament. The parliament's ability to review the decisions of the General Assembly would reinforce the Assembly's democratic authority. We might anticipate a shift of certain powers from the indirectly elected body to the directly elected one. We could begin, in other words, to see the development of a bicameral parliament for the planet, which starts to exercize some of the key functions of government.

The problem this scheme immediately encounters is that we can do nothing to change the way the United Nations works except at the behest of the five nations which control it. They can veto any attempt to remove their veto. They can use the UN Charter to prevent any changes to the Charter.

This appeared, until March 2003, to be an intractable problem. In the past, global security arrangements have been radically altered only in the wake of devastating world wars. But by shoving aside the Security Council in order to prosecute its war with Iraq, the United States may have begun to destroy the system which had formerly served it so well. By going to war without the council's authorization, and against the wishes of three of its permanent members and most of its temporary members, the US appears to have ceased even to *pretend* to play by the rules. If so, then the Security Council's residual claims to legitimacy and relevance will evaporate. It will lose its power of restraint. This would leave other nations with just two options.

The first is to accept that the security system has broken down and that disputes between nations will in future be resolved by means of bilateral diplomacy backed by force of arms. A world with no system would, as we would soon discover, be even crueller than a world with the wrong system. There would be no means of preventing the escalation of disputes and the possibility of world war. The second is to tear up the UN's constitution, override the US veto and build a new (and, we should hope, more democratic) global security system. This is a bold and dangerous strategy. The new system, just as the International Criminal Court and the Kyoto protocol on climate change have done, would have to begin without the involvement of the United States. The world's foremost military power would not then be party to the system of international law.

We could expect the US government to react with even greater hostility to this proposal than it has done towards the criminal court. The United States has tolerated the existing system only because it is undemocratic. A system which the US could neither veto nor easily reduce to an instrument of its foreign policy would be perceived as a threat to its power. The US government would then threaten to settle its disputes without reference to anybody else. So if a democratic security system, built on the weighted votes of the General Assembly, were to be devised, we would need either to persuade the United States to join and live by the rules, or to reduce its power to act outside the system. This second task is surely necessary whether the existing Security Council collapses or not.

It is important to remember here that the excesses of the US government do not suggest that there is anything the matter with the American people. Their government has behaved as any lone democratic superpower would behave. It is threatening simply because it is powerful. Part of the purpose of a democratic security system would be to prevent any nation from becoming so powerful again.

While the military power of the United States looks unchallengeable, it is, in other respects, far weaker than it might appear. Its vast national debt and budget deficit are sustainable only because the dollar has become the dominant international currency. As Chapter 5 will explain, the US obtains a massive subsidy from this arrangement. This is unlikely to last. In Europe, Russia and China the case for holding currency reserves in euros or yuan rather than dollars is being seriously considered. In 2000, Saddam Hussein insisted that Iraq's oil be purchased in euros, not dollars. Other oil producing states have, as the euro's value increases and their trade with Europe expands, powerful economic reasons to follow him. If they do, the international requirement for dollars could be greatly reduced. Indeed, the need to prevent this possibility might have been one of the reasons for the US government's determination to go to war with Iraq.[61] The rest of the world, in other words, has the means to wreck the US economy and, in doing so, to threaten its status as the global hegemon. This may be necessary if we are to construct a world order based on equity and justice.

We can expect our governments to seek every opportunity to duck these challenges. Confrontation with the superpower is something almost all of them have sought to avoid. I suspect, though, that oil traders, financial speculators and independent central banks will unwittingly begin to establish the financial pre-conditions for US containment on their behalf. Their courage will then be measured by their preparedness to seize the opportunity this creates. They will find this courage only if their electorates (led by a global justice movement which has, in many countries, given rise to and merged with the new peace campaigns) press home their duty to prevent the possibility of another world war.

CHAPTER 5

Something Snaps

An International Clearing Union

However successful our plans for democratic globalization may be, we can escape the need for internationalism only when nation states cease to exist. While they persist, we must assume that they and their institutions will continue, among other functions, to oversee the global flow of wealth. The wealth or poverty of peoples will remain affected by the strength or weakness of their national economies. This, in turn, will be affected by the relationship between them.

For the past 500 years, this relationship has been, essentially, predatory. The countries which as a result of various historical accidents were among the first to establish the international networks on which the current trading system was built, fashioned them to ensure that wealth flowed from their weaker trading partners into their own economies. By and large, this pattern has persisted, surviving both the transition from informal coercion to formal colonialism, and from colonialism back to informal coercion (a state of affairs generally described as 'independence').

There are two issues which must be understood if we are to see why some nations remain poor while others become rich. The first is the *conditions* under which nations trade with each other: namely the rules governing their exchanges, and the valuation of their resources. This (and the means of improving these conditions) is the theme of Chapter 6. The second is the *balance* of trade between nations, which is the theme of this chapter.

Though most people have failed to grasp this, much of the poor world's international debt is the result of uneven trade. If a nation wishes to buy goods from abroad, such as medicines or computers or grain, and has no foreign exchange with which to buy them, then it must borrow that money. It thus incurs an international debt. It can discharge that debt only by earning foreign exchange, which it seeks to do by exporting goods of its own. If it persistently fails to earn as much from its exports as it spends on its imports, its debt will begin to accumulate.* As this occurs, a nation must find more and more foreign money with which to pay

---

* A country which earns less than it spends is said to be in *deficit*. A country which earns more is in *surplus*. Because the global economy is a closed system (we do not trade with other planets), the total global surplus must be equivalent to the total global deficit.

the interest. This, unless it can boost the value of its exports, means that it must borrow still more, driving it further into debt. The further it falls into debt, and therefore the more it has to pay in interest, the less money it has to invest in building its economy and generating exports. It is easy to see, then, how the poorer nations become trapped in a vicious circle of debt.

The two international bodies which are supposed to help struggling economies both to avoid and to emerge from debt are the International Monetary Fund and the World Bank. That they have failed is not difficult to see; even after receiving debt relief, several poor nations are spending more on interest payments than on primary education.* Indeed the majority of their clients have fallen much further into debt than they were before these bodies intervened. While there is no question that some governments have contrib- uted generously to their nation's indebtedness through cor- ruption and mismanagement, those countries which have done precisely as the IMF and the Bank have instructed have found themselves becoming just as indebted as the countries condemned by these agencies as irresponsible. Indeed, it is demonstrable that the nations which have

---

* The current record is held by Sierra Leone, which spends 6.7 times more on servicing its debt than it spends on primary schooling. As a result, only twenty-four per cent of its children go to school. Debt payments consume nearly ninety per cent of the government's revenues.[62]

most obediently followed their prescriptions are among those which have suffered the most violent economic disruptions.

Just as the victors of the Second World War arranged the world's security systems to suit themselves, so the victors of the trade war being fought at the same time guaranteed that the world's international banking system reinforced and extended their power. The system they designed ensures that the further a weak nation falls into debt, the more it can be forced to do as they demand. Indebtedness, in other words, not only impoverishes a nation economically, but it also impoverishes a nation politically.

As this chapter will show, the IMF and the World Bank are both inherently unreformable and destined to fail. Indeed, their failure was predicted by many of the world's foremost economists at the time of their creation. Moreover, before they were established, a system widely recognized as far superior, in terms of both the efficiency of its operation and the justice of its likely outcomes, had already been designed. It was only through the exercise of extreme political pressure that this proposal was discarded in favour of the one we have today. We possess already the theoretical means by which trade can be balanced and international debt can be eliminated: not just once, but in perpetuity. We also, as I shall show, possess something even more interesting: the weapon required to overthrow the existing system and replace it with the one it usurped. This weapon is, I believe, irresistible. No government on earth, once we have learnt to use it, has the power to defend itself against us.

Such was the impact of his book that it would, perhaps, be appropriate to divide the public perception of the global justice movement into two periods: before and after Stiglitz. Before Joseph Stiglitz, the Nobel laureate who was formerly the chief economist of the World Bank and the chairman of the US president's Council of Economic Advisors, published the discoveries he had made during his terms of office,[63] the complaints of the movement were routinely dismissed by the rich world's pundits and politicians. After Stiglitz, even some of the market fundamentalists were forced to admit that our analysis was, in one respect, correct.

The intended purpose of the International Monetary Fund is to maintain global economic stability, by helping countries which have balance of payments problems; stabilizing exchange rates; and promoting economic growth, employment and workers' incomes. These duties would, its founders hoped, prevent the economic difficulties faced by one nation from infecting other nations, causing a global slump of the kind which established the preconditions for the Second World War. The IMF, Stiglitz shows, has in the past few years done precisely the opposite. By imposing policies designed to help the rich world's private banks and financial speculators rather than the poor world's struggling economies, it has destabilized exchange rates, exacerbated balance of payments problems, forced countries into debt and recession, and destroyed the jobs and incomes of tens of millions of workers.

The IMF's programmes, Stiglitz demonstrates, reflect 'the interests and ideology of the Western financial community'.[64] They are forced upon weaker nations regardless of their circumstances: every country the Fund instructs must place the control of inflation ahead of other economic objectives; immediately remove its barriers to trade and the flow of capital; liberalize its banking system; reduce government spending on everything except debt repayments; and privatize the assets which can be sold to foreign investors. These happen to be precisely the policies which suit the rich world's financial speculators. 'In a sense', Stiglitz writes, 'it is the IMF that keeps the speculators in business.' The weaker nations, knowing that the IMF can both cut off its own funds and recommend that private banks take the same action, are 'scared to disagree openly'. The Fund 'effectively stifles any discussions within a client government – let alone more broadly within the country – about alternative economic policies'. Citizens of those countries whose IMF programmes Stiglitz studied were 'not only barred from discussions of agreements; they were not even told what the agreements were'.[65]

In the 1980s the IMF began to destabilize some of the most successful economies in the developing world. Thailand, South Korea, the Philippines and Indonesia, in common with much of the rest of East Asia, had started to become rich by doing precisely what the IMF and World Bank had been telling them not to do. They had invested massively in education, and had actively promoted certain industries. They had been slow to remove the protective measures which permitted their own companies to develop before they were brought into direct competition with bigger businesses elsewhere. They had maintained their controls on the flows of speculative capital entering or leaving the economy. All of them had experienced huge rates of growth, which in nations such as South Korea and Thailand lifted most people out of poverty.

The IMF, working with the US Treasury and the bankers of Wall Street, and armed with the threat of its self-fulfilling prophecy (warning the financial markets that countries which did not do as it said were doomed), effectively forced those nations to drop their restrictions on the movements of capital. 'The countries in East Asia had no need for additional capital, given their high savings rate, but still capital account liberalization was pushed on these countries in the late eighties and early nineties. I believe that capital account liberalization was the single most important factor leading to the crisis . . . it is not just that the Fund pushed the liberalization policies which led to the crisis, but that they pushed these policies even though there was little evidence that such policies promoted growth, and there was ample evidence that they imposed huge risks on developing countries.'[66]

The result, as many people within those nations had predicted, was that their liberalized currencies began to be attacked by financial speculators. In 1997 they swooped on the region's most vulnerable currency, the Thai *baht*. They made their money by means of a simple speculative game. You borrow a huge quantity of *baht* from a Thai bank, while the currency is valuable. You convert the *baht* into dollars. If you do so suddenly enough and in sufficient quantity, the value of the currency collapses. *Baht*, as a result, are now much cheaper than they were before. You then pay off the loan with some of your dollars and pocket the difference. This is the business of some of the most admired 'investors' in the Western world. They have applied the ancient discipline of peculation, and respectabilized it by prefixing an 's'. It is made possible by the IMF's insistence on capital market liberalization.

Having wrecked Thailand's currency, the IMF then poured billions of dollars in the form of loans into the country, ostensibly 'to support the exchange rate'. Precisely as its critics predicted, almost all this money was sucked straight back out of the country, as Western banks recovered their loans and national elites moved their investments into other nations. It repeated this approach in all the Asian countries whose currencies were smashed by speculators, to the great benefit of the foreign banks. The loans left those crippled nations no better off than they were before, but with massive new debts. As these countries teetered on the brink of catastrophe, the IMF kept shoving. First it 'talked down' the threatened economies, then it forced them into recession by demanding that they raise their interest rates to extraordinary levels. This, predictably enough, bankrupted many of their indebted companies, and the bankruptcies, in turn, started pulling down the banks. Foreign corporations, most of them based in the United States, sharked in and started buying the bankrupted firms for a fraction of their value. As if to distribute the economic contagion as rapidly as possible, the IMF, in the midst of the recession it had induced, forced the affected countries to balance their budgets. This meant that they had to cut their imports, with the inevitable result that their trading partners (principally the other countries in the region) began to lose their exports.

By 1998, the International Monetary Fund had spread the disaster it had caused as far as Russia, which was heavily dependent on exports to the emerging economies and was already suffering from the Fund's bad advice. The IMF then applied the same formula for 'recovery' to Russia's sick economy, and very nearly precipitated a complete global collapse. It had, Stiglitz notes, caused 'the greatest economic crisis since the Great Depression'. As I write, it appears to be pushing Latin America in the same direction, having forced Argentina to reduce its spending as it went into recession, neatly transforming a downturn into a disaster.

The East Asian countries which survived the crash were those which refused to listen to the IMF. Malaysia did just what the Fund told it not to do: it maintained its controls on the flow of capital. This, Stiglitz remarks, 'allowed it to recover more quickly' from the regional recession, 'with a shallower downturn, and with a far smaller legacy of national debt burdening future growth ... Today Malaysia stands in a far better position than those countries that took IMF advice.'[67] China too retained its capital controls, and its economy grew by eight per cent per year while most of those in the region contracted. Similar comparisons can be made between Russia, which did as the IMF instructed and collapsed, and Poland, which refused to take the IMF's advice and prospered.

These crises and related disasters, triggered or exacerbated by the IMF, have thrown tens of millions of people out of work, turned comfortable citizens into poor ones and poor citizens into desperate ones, destroyed investment in education, health and other public services, undermined the ability of nations to feed themselves, and provoked riots in just about every country in which the Fund has worked. The only clear beneficiaries of its programmes have been foreign banks and corporations, speculative investors and some members of the domestic elite. 'While the IMF had provided some \$23 billion [to the East Asian governments] to be used to support the exchange rate and bail out creditors,' Stiglitz notes, 'the far, far smaller sums required to help the poor were not forthcoming. In American parlance, there were billions and billions for corporate welfare, but not the more modest millions for welfare for ordinary citizens.'[68]

Stiglitz's book suffers from two major omissions. He fails to propose viable solutions to the problems he documents. And, perhaps because he is, in his gentlemanly fashion, concerned not to appear to be suffering from sour grapes, he fails rigorously to examine the role of his former employers, the World Bank.* For while the Bank appears to have been a little more prepared to listen to its critics, its policies have been almost as destructive as those of the IMF. The World Bank's original purpose was to provide long-term loans to the nations whose economies had been devastated by the Second World War. This was a useful and important role, and for the first few years of its existence the Bank plainly did more good than harm. But, without the consent of the countries in which it works, its mandate has steadily expanded. Among the other duties it has awarded itself are providing 'project aid' for building dams or planting cash crops, 'adjustment loans' intended to help countries pay their debts, and loan guarantees to corporations, many of which are based in the rich world. As its responsibilities have expanded and the demands of the rich world have become more pressing, its destructive impacts have come

---

* Stiglitz found that he had no option but to resign, after he was prevented by the Bank from speaking out.

to outweigh the good it does. The World Bank has unintentionally become one of the poor world's major causes of poverty, environmental destruction and debt.

By contrast to the IMF, which appears to remain impervious to experience, every few years the Bank admits that some of its policies have been disastrous, and that it needs to change the way it works. It then changes the names of its programmes, rewrites its stated objectives, and continues to operate much as it did before. It appears to accept, for example, that many of the hydro-electric dams it sponsored, whose purpose was to relieve poverty and generate wealth, have forced hundreds of thousands of people to leave their land, destroyed natural resources and cost the recipient countries far more money than they made, adding to their burden of debt. Yet, from Laos to Uganda, it continues to assist hydro-electric projects with identical problems. It seems to agree with its critics that its 'adjustment lending' encourages deforestation, and yet its revised forest policy, just like the old one, fails properly to address this impact.[69] It knows that forcing a country to reduce its spending during a recession will drive its economy further into recession, yet, alongside the IMF, it has forced Argentina to do just this. The World Bank is prepared to learn from experience, only to discard that learning in favour of the strategies it knows have failed.

While much of its project funding has contributed significantly to poverty by demanding impossible rates of return, it is the Bank and the IMF's 'adjustment lending' which has locked many nations into destitution. The loans the Bank makes are supposed to help a country pay its debts, while restructuring its economy to discourage government profligacy and attract investors. In order to receive this assistance a government must agree to certain 'conditionalities'. These conditionalities, which often involve a massive reduction in government spending on public services, the sale of public assets, the privatization of state food reserves and state marketing boards for staple crops and the laying off of workers, represent a complete reversal of the World Bank's original objectives: to boost public services, reduce hunger and bring more people into employment. They are indirectly responsible for hundreds of thousands of deaths.

Indebted nations have been forced to reduce their spending on health and education. In many of the countries in which the World Bank and IMF have worked, people must now pay for these services. The results are catastrophic. In Kenya, for example, one of the countries worst affected by AIDS, the number of women seeking help or advice on sexually transmitted diseases declined by sixty-five per cent following the introduction of fees.[70] In Ghana, the new fees forced two-thirds of rural families to stop sending their children to school.[71] The cuts in health spending the Bank and the IMF forced on Zambia helped to increase infant mortality from ninety-seven deaths per 1000 births in 1980 to 202 deaths per 1000 in 1999.[72]

The World Bank now claims that the bad old days of restructuring are over. Instead of imposing 'structural adjustment programmes' on the indebted nations, it now permits them to design their own 'poverty reduction strategies'. This sounds like an improvement, until you discover that the poverty reduction strategies are just as coercive as the structural adjustment programmes. As one senior official at the Bank revealed, the new scheme is a 'compulsory programme, so that those with the money can tell those without the money what they need in order to get the money'.[73] And what they have to do, yet again, is to open their economies to foreign banks and corporations and reduce state spending on almost everything except the repayment of debt. The debt relief programme which the Bank and the Fund claim will rescue the nations with the most desperate economic problems – the 'Highly Indebted Poor Countries Initiative' – imposes still fiercer conditionalities, while relieving only part of the debt.*

It is a cause of bitter mirth in the poor world that among the conditionalities the IMF and World Bank demand are 'good governance' and 'democratization'. Their own governance of the economies of the poor nations could scarcely be more damaging, while in terms of accountability, trans-

---

* In 2001, for example, nineteen of the twenty-six countries which qualified for relief under the HIPC initiative still had to spend over ten per cent of government revenue on servicing their debt.[74]

parency and the ability of their subject peoples to dislodge them by peaceful means, they are about as democratic as the government of Burma. The nations they control, and in which they claim to be encouraging 'democratization', are permitted to choose only one political and economic strategy: market fundamentalism. It is imposed with a zeal which, at times, appears totalitarian.

They work like this because, though they operate upon the poor, they are controlled by the rich. The bigger a nation's economy, and therefore the greater its share of the institutions' funds, the more votes it can cast. The 'G8' nations – that is the United States, Canada, Japan, Russia, the United Kingdom, France, Germany and Italy – possess forty-nine per cent of the votes within the IMF[75] and (averaged across its four principal agencies) forty-eight per cent of the votes within the World Bank.* While these figures suggest that the power of eight of their 184 members is disproportionate, they make these bodies look rather more democratic than they are, for they create the impression that if the rest of the world pooled its votes, it could turn a decision against the richest nations. The constitution of both bodies ensures

---

* This breaks down as follows. In the International Bank for Reconstruction and Development, the G8 has 45.9 per cent of the vote, in the International Finance Corporation, 55.3 per cent, in the International Development Association, 48.6 per cent and in the Multilateral Investment Guarantee Agency, 43.3 per cent.[76]

that all major decisions require an eighty-five per cent majority. The US alone possesses seventeen per cent of the votes in the IMF,[77] and averaged across its agencies, eighteen per cent of the votes in the World Bank.* By itself, in other words, it can veto any substantial resolution put forward by another country, even if all the other members support it.

Just in case the poorer countries somehow fail to get the message, the managing director of the IMF is always a European, and his deputy is always a North American,[79] while the president of the World Bank is always a citizen of the United States,[80] nominated by the US Treasury Secretary.[81] Both institutions are based in Washington DC.

The result is that there is one rule for the rich and one for the poor. While the poor nations are forced to beggar themselves to pay their unpayable debts, the world's biggest international debtor, the United States, which owes a total of $2.2 trillion, is left to its own devices: it suffers from no externally imposed austerity programmes, inflation control or forced liberalization. Indeed, one of the reasons why America's indebtedness has not resulted in its economic collapse is that the IMF and World Bank insist that the foreign exchange reserves other nations maintain to defend

---

* 16.5 per cent in the IBRD, 14.6 per cent in the IDA, 23.7 per cent in the IFC and 16.4 per cent in the MIGA.[78]

themselves from speculative attacks are held in the form of dollars. This reinforces the dollar's position as the dominant international currency, artificially enhances its value, and permits the United States to reap three significant subsidies from poorer nations.[82] The first arises from the fact that dollar reserves must be invested in assets in the United States, which boosts US capital accounts. The second is that poorer nations must pay around eighteen per cent interest on the dollars they borrow, yet they lend them back to the US at three per cent.[83] The third is that a government issuing currency obtains what is known as *seignorage*: the difference between the value of that currency and the cost of producing it. Not only are the IMF and the World Bank helping to destroy the economies of weaker nations, but they are also helping to sustain the economic dominance, and therefore the political hegemony, of the United States.

Over the past sixty years, there have been scores of well-meaning proposals to reform these bodies, by redistributing their votes and changing their constitutions. They may as well be calling for a change in the orbit of the earth. For what all these proposals overlook, with a blitheness which must at times be wilful, is that the veto the US exercises over major decisions is also a *constitutional* veto: nothing can change unless it agrees to that change. The World Bank and the IMF are as rigidly controlled as the United Nations Security Council.

*   *   *

But even if the nations that run these institutions acted in good faith, they could scarcely improve the lives of the poor, for both the World Bank and the International Monetary Fund are constitutionally destined to fail. The reason for this is simple: they place the entire burden of maintaining the balance of international trade on the nations least able to affect it, by which I mean the debtors. These countries must discharge their debts by engineering a massive trade surplus, even though with weak currencies, deficient infrastructure and public services and no money for investment, they are in a poor position to do so. The world economy, controlled by the rich nations, is stacked against the poor. As a result, those who control the World Bank and the IMF have long ceased to pretend that they are helping them to emerge from debt, but instead seek only to ensure that their debts are paid, by shifting their natural resources overseas. They have become the bailiffs of the world economy, the global equivalent of the people who take away your television when you haven't paid your bills.

Nor do these institutions have any incentive to change the way they work. As the World Bank official Steen Jorgensen told a meeting of NGOs at the Bank's summit in Prague, 'If we cancel the debt there will be no World Bank. The World Bank pays my salary.'[84]

There is no prospect that the world's impoverished nations will ever discharge their debts. They owe a total of $2.5 trillion, largely to commercial banks and the World

Bank and IMF. Between 1980 and 1996, the nations of sub-Saharan Africa paid twice the sum of their total debt in the form of interest, but they still owed three times more in 1996 than they did in 1980.[85] The lending by the World Bank, which was supposed to help nations to pay their debts, has itself become a major cause of debt, as the Bank has put its money into schemes which could never have paid for themselves, let alone generated extra revenues. Even those indebted nations which have been able to establish a trade surplus and sustain it for several years have discovered that the money has scarcely been sufficient to pay the interest, let alone to begin discharging the principal.* The debt, as the governments of the rich world now appear to accept, is unpayable.

This accumulation of debt has been accompanied by a massive transfer of natural resources from the poor world to the rich world. If these resources were valued according to their utility, the nations of the poor world would surely be the creditors, and the nations of the rich world the debtors. As the Native American leader Guaicaipuro Cuautemoc has pointed out, between 1503 and 1660, 185,000 kilogrammes of gold and 16 million kilogrammes of silver were shipped from Latin America to Europe. Cuautemoc argues that his people should see this transfer not as a war crime, but as 'the first of several friendly loans, granted by America

---

* The principal is the original sum they were lent.

for Europe's development'. Were the indigenous people of Latin America to charge compound interest on this loan, at the modest rate of ten per cent, Europe would owe them a volume of gold and silver which exceeded the weight of the planet.[86]

That the colonized world, whose wealth has been plundered for 500 years, should be deemed to owe the rich world money, and that this presumed debt should be so onerous that every year $382 billion, which might have been used to feed the hungry, to house the poor, to provide healthcare, education, clean water, transport and pensions for people who have access to none of these amenities, is transferred from the poor world to the banks and financial institutions of the rich world in the form of debt repayments[87] is an obscenity which degrades all those of us who benefit from it. It is an obscenity perpetuated by the very system which was, or so we are told, designed to bring it to an end.

One of the more interesting discoveries I have made while researching this book is the near absence of historical awareness on all sides of the debate. Few of those who criticize the international institutions, and few of those who work for them, appear to have any idea of how they came about and why they take the form they do. Partly as a result, the debate has been characterized by a profound ignorance of the alternatives.

There is no better example of this than the prevailing misconception about the origins of the World Bank and the International Monetary Fund. Almost everyone appears to believe that they were founded by the brilliant liberal economist John Maynard Keynes. In his pamphlet attacking the global justice movement, for example, the journalist John Lloyd claims that Keynes was 'the most important theorist behind the creation of the international bodies' (the IMF and the World Bank).[88] Even the great Joe Stiglitz, who was, of course, the World Bank's chief economist, describes Keynes as 'the intellectual godfather of the IMF'. He suggests that 'Keynes would be rolling over in his grave were he to see what has happened to his child'.[89] In fact, poor Lord Keynes would be rolling over in his grave were he to see how badly he has been misrepresented.

The agreement which led to the establishment of the IMF and the World Bank was brokered, in 1944, in a hotel beside a deserted railway stop called Bretton Woods, in New Hampshire in the United States. Today the Bretton Woods Agreement is perceived as the rich world's solution to the poor world's problems, but its principal concern was the reconstruction of Europe after the war. Indeed the debtor nation facing the most urgent balance of payments problems was not Mozambique, or Tanzania or Indonesia, all of which were then European colonies, but Britain.

The conference was, in essence, a battle between two remarkable men. One of them was Harry Dexter White, the head of the US negotiating team, an ingenious policy-maker and brutally adept negotiator, whose ideas had come to dominate the thinking of the US Treasury. The other was the head of the British team, John Maynard Keynes, almost universally recognized as the greatest economist of his day. The United States was then, as it is today, the world's dominant economic power. Britain, largely as a result of the war, was a major debtor nation which happened to contain an economic genius charged with trying to rescue its economy. What he devised, though we have been remarkably slow to see it, was a system which could not have been better designed to address the still graver problems faced by the poor nations today.

Keynes recognized that debtor nations can do little to affect the balance of trade. They can reduce the value of their currencies in the hope of making their exports more attractive, but all that then happens is that the value of their exports falls at the same rate as the volume increases. This problem, Keynes saw, is compounded by two others. The first is that a heavily indebted nation must spend much of the money it possesses on paying its debts. There is, therefore, less available to invest in businesses which could generate exports, with the result that the trade deficit is likely to increase as the debt grows. The second problem is that the money shifted around the world by financial speculators tends to leave nations which are in financial trouble, and enter nations which are prospering, meaning that the debtor nations have even less to invest in generating exports, while the creditor nations have more and more. Both sets of countries, then, are locked into their economic positions: the debtors are destined to become poorer and fall further into debt, while the creditors are destined to accumulate ever more of the world's money.

Keynes came to the obvious conclusion that the terms of trade between nations cannot be substantially affected unless the creditors as well as the debtors are obliged to change them. His solution was an ingenious system for persuading the creditor nations to spend their surplus money back into the economies of the debtor nations. He suggested that a global bank, which he called the International Clearing Union, should be established. This bank would issue its own currency, which he named the *bancor*. The bancor, which was exchangeable with national currencies at fixed rates of exchange, would be the unit of account between nations: it would be used, in other words, to measure a country's trade deficit or trade surplus.* Every country would have an overdraft facility in its bancor account at the International Clearing Union, equivalent to half the average value of its trade over the past five years. As all the deficits and surpluses in global trade add up, by definition, to zero, the overdrafts would, in aggregate, be equal to the surpluses.

---

* I am grateful to Michael Rowbotham, whose book *Goodbye America!: Globalisation, Debt and the Dollar Empire*[90] introduced me to this proposal.

All the members of the Union would discover that they had a powerful incentive, by the end of the year, to 'clear' their bancor accounts; that is, to end up with zero, meaning that they had accumulated, when everything was added up, neither a trade deficit nor a trade surplus across the year. The incentive arose from a remarkably simple device. Any central bank using more than half of its overdraft allowance (in other words, going too far into trade deficit) would be charged interest on its overdraft, which would rise as its overdraft rose. It would also be obliged to reduce the value of its currency by up to five per cent (making its exports more attractive) and to prevent the export of capital. These are conventional means of discouraging excessive debt.

But – and this was Keynes's key innovation – the nations with a trade surplus would be subject to almost identical pressures. Any member nation with a bancor credit balance which was more than half the size of its overdraft facility would be charged interest on that account at the rate of ten per cent.* It would also be obliged to increase the value of its currency and to permit the export of capital. If, by the end of the year, its credit balance exceeded the total value of its permitted overdraft, the surplus would be confiscated. All these surpluses and interest payments would be placed in the Clearing Union's Reserve Fund.[91]

---

* The proper term for 'negative interest' of this kind is *demurrage*.

These rules, then, would change how nations with a trade surplus operate, in three ways. Their exports would become less attractive, because the value of their currencies would rise if they went beyond a certain level of surplus. Capital would not flee from nations in major deficit into nations in major surplus because its movements would be blocked in that direction, but not in the other. Most importantly, a country with a trade surplus would seek to minimize it by introducing domestic policies to encourage its citizens and businesses to increase the value of their imports. Governments themselves could use their surplus bancors to buy goods from overseas. This means, in aggregate, that the nations in surplus would spend their money back into the deficit nations.

What Keynes had designed was a system which automatically prevented the vicious circle from turning. Deficit nations would be brought back to equilibrium, and so would the surplus nations. Instead of temporary debts leading to permanent debts, and small debts leading to big ones, credit and debit would cancel each other out by the end of every year. The economic and political power of the creditor nations would no longer accumulate, just as the present weakness of the debtor nations would no longer drive them further into dependency.

Keynes had begun to develop this thinking in 1931, but it was not until 1941 that he had devised a coherent system. As he refined the argument and began to circulate his papers in 1942 and 1943, his idea detonated in the minds of all who read it. The British economist Lionel Robbins recorded that 'it would be difficult to exaggerate the electrifying effect on thought throughout the whole relevant apparatus of government of the production of this document . . . nothing so imaginative and so ambitious had ever been discussed as a possibility of responsible government policy . . . it became as it were a banner of hope, an inspiration to the daily grind of war-time duties.'[92]

Britain's European allies were similarly enthusiastic. Economists everywhere began to see that Keynes had cracked it: he had, for the first time in history, devised a distributive system which increased the general prosperity, while levelling the power of nations. Its contribution to peace and the balance of power could prove to be just as decisive as its contribution to the balance of trade. As the Allies prepared for the conference to be held at Bretton Woods, Britain adopted Keynes's solution as its official negotiating position, and he was appointed to lead the British delegation.

The nation in which his project was received with less enthusiasm was the United States. The US was the world's biggest creditor, and it was determined to stay that way. The war had greatly boosted its exports, and it was concerned that without an aggressive trade policy, peace could lead to recession. Harry Dexter White ruled out any possibility that the surplus nations should be required to alter the terms of trade: 'We have been perfectly adamant on that point. We have taken the position of absolutely no, on that.'[93] Other nations were left in little doubt about where their interests lay. Keynes noted that the opinion of the European allies, South America and the British Commonwealth 'is strongly and predominantly in favour of the Clearing Union. On the other hand, many of those concerned are extremely timid about opposing the USA, seeing that they have what I believe are known as "expectations".[94] Britain's relationship with the US was also extremely unequal, as it had become dependent on the larger economy to provide the resources required to win the war. By the summer of 1943, it was clear that Keynes's solution would not be permitted to prevail.

Harry Dexter White had proposed an alternative plan, for an 'International Stabilization Fund' and an 'International Bank for Reconstruction and Development'. The Stabilization Fund would maintain steady exchange rates, reduce foreign exchange controls and lend money to nations in deficit. The Bank would provide the capital needed by allied countries for economic reconstruction after the war. The Fund placed the entire burden of maintaining the balance of trade on the deficit nations. The more they borrowed from the International Stabilization Fund, the higher the interest rates would become. There were no limits to the surplus that successful exporters could accumulate. The International Stabilization Fund became the

International Monetary Fund. The International Bank for Reconstruction and Development remains the principal lending arm of the World Bank.

White insisted that 'the more money you put in, the more votes you have'.[95] As a result, all the nations at the conference argued that they should be allowed a bigger quota of contributions to the two bodies. But White's team had already allocated them. 'The US', he decided, 'should have enough votes to block any decision.'[96]

White demanded that national debts be redeemable for gold, that gold be convertible into dollars at the fixed rate of $35 an ounce, and that all exchange rates be fixed against the dollar. This effectively established the hegemony of the dollar as the unit of account between nations, not least because, twenty-seven years later, the US reneged on the agreement and suspended the convertibility of gold into dollars. Though the other nations objected furiously, White also decided that both the Fund and the Bank would be sited in Washington.

Keynes knew that his own proposal was, for the purposes of the conference, dead, and that the best he could do was to seek to modify the competing plan. He managed to manoeuvre himself into the position of the conference's chair, which is perhaps why he is so often and so erroneously credited with the formation of the bodies which were approved at Bretton Woods. As US records show, however, the United States not only possessed all the necessary powers, but, by laying down the conference procedures, it also ensured that its proposals could not be effectively challenged. The historian Armand van Dormael has studied the minutes of the US delegation's planning meetings.[97] The negotiators appear to have agreed, he found, that 'anybody can talk as long as he pleases provided he doesn't say anything. Separate the business of the Committee from the talk', and that they should 'go through the motions' in pretending to consider the alternatives.[98] White also prided himself on having drafted his proposition so that it appeared to mean one thing but in fact meant quite another. In short, the US deployed all the usual deceptions and evasions of international diplomacy. The problem was that the other nations were in no position to challenge it with deceptions and evasions of their own.

Keynes resisted some of the details of White's plan till the end, and continued to insist that there would, one day, have to be some mechanism for balancing exports and imports. He won a few short-lived concessions for Britain, such as measures restricting currency speculation. But, though he knew it could not solve the underlying problems, he signed the agreement because he also knew that a system based on rules, even the wrong rules, was better than a system with no rules at all. As his biographer Robert Skidelsky notes, 'Keynes gave the Bretton Woods Agreement its distinction not its substance. The agreement reflected the views of the American, not the British Treasury, of White not Keynes. The British contribution tended, finally, towards the negotiation of derogations, postponements and escape clauses.'[99] The Americans had won, and engineered a perfect formula for both continued US economic dominance and the permanent indebtedness of the poor nations. It is profoundly ironic that, four years later, Harry Dexter White was charged with un-American activities.*

Back in Britain, as Michael Rowbotham records, Keynes tried bravely to defend the outcome of the conference to the British people. He was forced to concede, however, in a letter to *The Times*, that some of the policies agreed at Bretton Woods 'may . . . be very foolish' and 'destructive of international trade'.[100] The British parliament was told that if it didn't accept the new system, the US would withhold its next war loan. But few economists were in any doubt about what the outcome would be. Sir Edward Holloway, for example, predicted that the American system would lead to 'unpayable indebtedness between nations'.[101] Geoffrey Crowther, the editor of the *Economist*, a magazine which now defends the way the World Bank and IMF are constituted, warned that 'Lord Keynes was right . . . the world will bit-

---

* On 31 July and 3 August 1948, White was accused of being, respectively, a Soviet infiltrator and a Communist agent in testimony by Soviet spies to the House Committee on Un-American Activities. He was called before the committee on 13 August, and died three days later.

terly regret the fact that his arguments were rejected.'[102] I think we can fairly conclude that these warnings have been vindicated.

Sixty years on, the case for an International Clearing Union, or a body built on similar principles, appears to be stronger than ever. The predictions made by Keynes and other prominent economists have come true, and the evidence that the IMF and the World Bank are not working confronts anyone who is not deliberately disregarding it. In some respects, Keynes's idea needs to be refined and updated – and several models have been suggested – but the basic brainwork has been done by an economist perhaps more able than any the world can offer today. We do not have to invent a wholly novel system.

A few modifications appear to be self-evident. Keynes proposed that his Clearing Union be managed by eight governors, drawn from the major trading blocs. The United States, Britain, the British Empire, the Soviet Union and Latin America would each supply one and the rest of Europe would provide two, while the eighth seat went to somewhere unspecified. Today, we might hope that the seats would be distributed rather more equitably.

It is also clear, as Michael Rowbotham has pointed out, that the total number of bancors in the accounts of member nations will always be less than zero, because at any one time part of the currency will be active: in other words engaged in transactions or clearances. To avoid the danger of aggregate debt, we would have to issue enough extra bancors in the form of free currency to ensure that there is an overall balance of trade. This may seem like a minor point, but, as I will show below, it appears to me to have some interesting consequences.

Thanks to the operation of 'leveraged hedge funds' (the speculators who borrow a vulnerable currency, then dump it to force down its value) and other modern forms of financial speculation, there now seems to be a case for more sweeping and frequent controls on the movement of capital than Keynes envisaged. Global flows of 'hot money' are devastating not only to economies but also to democracy. The governments of nations whose capital markets have been liberalized soon discover that they can pursue only those policies which don't 'upset the markets'. In practice, the demands of financial speculators are even more exacting than those of the IMF.

In Brazil, for example, a few months before Lula's election in 2002, the IMF demanded that the nation maintain a 'primary budget surplus' of 3.75 per cent, which is another way of saying that it would not permit any candidate significantly to raise social spending, despite the desperate needs of the nation's poorer citizens. But the markets demanded between four and five per cent. All the candidates knew what this meant. If they spent any more than these limits allowed, the speculators would wreak such economic havoc that their government would collapse. When a confederacy of exalted thieves in Wall Street, Tokyo and the City of London, whose interests are precisely opposed to those of the people of the nations they plunder, can tell those nations what their economic policies will be, democracy is reduced to a dress code. A modern Clearing Union, then, would permit – perhaps would encourage – nations to impose such controls on the movement of capital as were necessary to prevent the banks from running the world.

The gift which Keynes has offered us, and which we have so far refused to accept, is a world in which the poor nations are neither condemned to do as the rich nations say, nor condemned to stay poor. A Clearing Union releases weak nations from the deficit trap, in which they must seek to produce an ever greater volume of exports in the hope of generating a sustained trade surplus, even while other, more powerful nations are trying to do the same. It ensures that demand for their exports is mobilized when it is most needed, and that nations are obliged to cooperate. Instead of seeking to beggar each other by simultaneously pursuing a trade surplus, those nations in surplus will, if the mechanism works, voluntarily go into deficit just as the deficit nations need to go into surplus. Instead of demanding an impossible world, the Escher's staircase envisaged by the IMF and the World Bank, in which all nations simultaneously outcompete all others, it recognizes that balance can be achieved only if some nations' trade accounts descend while others rise.

One of the implications of this is that nations will need to trade less in order to stay afloat. A self-balancing international trading system is likely to bring an end to desperate overproduction by the poor and (because commodities are, as a result, so cheap) massive overconsumption by the rich. It goes some way, in other words, towards solving the environmental crisis propelled by the existing trade system, as a result both of the destruction of soil, water supplies and habitats caused by the ever-expanding extraction of commodities and of the global climate change exacerbated by the transport of these excessive goods. Interestingly, it begins to meet this need without any reliance on 'localization'.

Keynes's system also removes the means by which the rich nations can dictate economic policy to the poor. So accustomed are we to the notion that the poor world must do as 'the Washington consensus' requires that we find it almost inconceivable that a system could be introduced which permitted governments to act in the interests of their people. But the Clearing Union, or an updated and amended version of it, involves no forced liberalization, no 'conditionalities', no engineering of opportunities for predatory banks and corporations, no trampling of democratic consent. It is a system built on the notion of equality between trading partners, rather than that principle implicit in the constitution of the existing bodies: the tyranny of the founder.

The Union also provides us with something of use to some of our other projects, namely cash. We have seen that to prevent the system from succumbing to aggregate debt, a quantity of 'free money' in the form of bancors would need to be released. This money obtains value only if it is spent into circulation. It is likely to amount to the equivalent of some tens of billions of dollars, exchangeable into local currencies at the rates set by the Clearing Union's governing body.* While such funds would doubtless attract competing claims – national governments could be expected, for example, to suggest that they each receive a share – a strong case could be made for their expenditure on a project of benefit to the world's people. One such proposal is the first global election.

You may also recall that Keynes's system envisages the creation of a 'Reserve Fund', into which the interest payments incurred by both deficit and surplus nations and the confiscated assets of the nations with excessive credit balances would be placed. Keynes was not slow to grasp the potential of this fund. He suggested that it be used to finance a world police force and to provide the necessary money

---

* Or, if it were deemed more appropriate by the governors, the floating rates determined by a market regulated by the policies of national governments.

for disaster relief and reconstruction in countries that find themselves in trouble. We could anticipate that this fund, by comparison to existing sources of aid, would be enormous: quite big enough to finance both our parliament and its subsequent elections and those operations and proposals of the United Nations which have suffered so gravely for want of cash. While many sources of new money for global projects have been suggested – such as tax on financial transactions, use of the IMF's special drawing rights and a global lottery – none is so equitable, so reliable and so substantial as Keynes's reserve fund.

By now you are, I hope, nodding and shaking your head with equal vigour. Yes, this system could work, but how on earth could it be implemented? Given that the world's most powerful government blocked it in 1943 and has just as great an interest in blocking it today; given that the IMF and World Bank are constitutionally unreformable, how do we overthrow the system which works for the powerful and replace it with one which works for the weak? I believe I have the answer. It is the very injustice of the existing system which has provided the poor nations with the weapon required to overturn it. That weapon is their debt.

It would be misleading to make a direct comparison between the size of the poor world's debt – some $2.5 trillion – and the size of the combined reserves of all the world's central banks: some $1.3 trillion. Much of the debt has already been 'discounted': its real value to the banks which issued it, or to the 'secondary debt' traders who have bought it, is less than its paper value. As most of the debt is not a debt between governments, but a debt between governments and the commercial banks and the IMF and the World Bank, several intermediaries and complicating factors inhibit the translation of the banks' liabilities into national stocks of gold and dollars. Even so, the figures provide us with a rough idea of both the size of the weapon, and the incapacity of any government or financial institution to resist it, which has been handed to the poor by the rapacity of the rich. The poor world owns the rich world's banks.

Over the past sixty years, citizens of the poor world have often urged their governments to default on their debts: to announce, in other words, that they had no intention of paying. Some, recognizing the rich world's ability both to withstand a single default and to punish the defaulter (as Mexico was punished for its insubordination in 1982), have advocated that their nations coordinate their default: that all of them dump their debts at once. Had they done so, they would have thrown away their only effective weapon before it had fired a shot. They would have shed their debt, but done nothing to change the system which would ensure that it immediately began to re-accumulate. Instead, the poor world should do as the IMF and the World Bank have done, and attach 'conditionalities' to the handling of its debt. Just as the IMF has threatened to ruin the economies of the poor nations if they do not implement the reforms it demands, the poor world should threaten to ruin the economies of the rich nations if they do not agree to its terms. The point of possessing a terrifying weapon is that you do not have to use it; the fear of the weapon is sufficient to ensure that other people do as you demand. Nowhere does fear do its work with more celerity and less constraint than in the financial markets, which often flee even from their own shadows.

The financial system is built on a fantasy: that the debts on which it has constructed its wealth will one day be redeemed. The possibility that it could be awoken from its dream, that the nations which own the banks might dump the debt on which the system is built, would induce a panic that no financial market could resist. The enemies of the poor will be forced to turn upon each other. The banks and financial speculators of the rich world, who have, through the liberalization of financial markets, been granted power over their own governments, will, when they realize that the developing nations are serious, demand that the rich world's governments must do as the poor world requests, to prevent the entire structure's collapse. Thus all the means which have been deployed by the rich against the poor are neatly turned around and deployed by the poor against the rich.

Of course, for the threat to be effective, it would have to be a real one. The indebted nations would have to be prepared to implement it, in the unlikely event that the markets did not do as they wished. If they did fire this gun, they could expect their own economies to be shaken as much as those of the rich world: their chronic crisis would be compressed into an acute one. But for many of them, this is happening anyway, as an impending global recession and the demands of the IMF and the speculators render the debt burden still less supportable. There are several governments in Latin America, Africa and Asia which may be prepared to jump before they are pushed. We can expect the governments of the rich world to threaten every kind of retribution, but they will be able to enact such punishments only if the poor world is divided. If it sticks together, the rich world cannot harm it without further harming itself.

There is no better use for this weapon than to demolish the system which forged it. By holding the world to ransom, the indebted nations can demand the replacement of the IMF and the World Bank with an arrangement which automatically establishes a balance of trade. It is blackmail of course, but blackmail of precisely the kind the strong have used to subdue the weak for the past sixty years. The poor would thus offer the rest of the world a choice: it can opt either for a soft landing – a gentle transition from the existing system to the new one, and a staggered redemption of the debts accumulated as a result of the IMF's past mismanagement – or a crash landing. The markets will demand the soft one. Both courses of action will lead to the cancellation of debt. One of them, the crash landing, will internationalize the financial crisis already afflicting many of the indebted countries. The other will introduce a system which, while denying the G8 nations their control of the rest of the world, will provide for a more stable global economy, less prone to the cycle of boom and bust, while permitting everyone on earth a decent quality of life. The poor nations need not wait for the rich to establish a Clearing Union. They can found it themselves, fix the value of their currencies against the bancor (or whatever they might call it), then invite the rich countries, at the point of their financial gun, to join.

The debtor governments will not act without the most vexatious demands from their people. Most of them, through the elimination of alternatives, were effectively chosen by the IMF and the speculators. We can expect them to resist the proposals presented here; many will have to be overthrown in favour of those which are prepared to act on behalf of their people. But even radical governments will respond only if their people exert at least as much pressure as the IMF and the rich nations do. In some of the poor nations, the IMF's decisions feature almost daily in the newspapers. Everyone knows what 'structural adjustment' is and understands what it is doing to their lives. It is not hard to see how the demand that the government fights back, fuelled by the hope which a viable alternative encourages, could become the key political issue on which national elections are won or lost.

Indeed this, in many nations, is already the case. 'IMF riots' have shaken most of the countries which the Fund has graced with its attentions, and several governments have fallen over the past ten years as a result of the policies it has forced them to adopt. Almost everyone in the governments of the indebted nations I have spoken to agrees that they cannot go on as they are: the interest is unpayable, the demands of the creditors too onerous, the forbearance of their people tested beyond political limits. Something has to snap. One of the reasons why these governments have not turned their domestic difficulties into a concerted campaign against the source of the problem is that they have not been presented with a viable alternative, as almost everyone has forgotten about Keynes.

Once it is plain that several of the indebted nations are prepared to use this weapon, the threat of default could become contagious, as other countries find safety in numbers. As the rich world seeks to split the debtors' coalition by buying or bludgeoning some of its members, the citizens of these countries will need to press their demands with enterprise and perseverance. The struggle is dangerous, and the outcome uncertain. But if the people of the poor world do not rebel against the impositions of the rich, there is no uncertainty about the outcome. Many of them have a straightforward choice: to fight or to starve.

As the citizens of the indebted nations realize that the existing system offers them no remission, they will fight.

At length, their governments will buckle to their demands, because they too will have no choice. Unrealistic as this prescription might at first have appeared, it seems, on reflection, to be rather more plausible than a perpetuation of the present order.

CHAPTER 6

The Levelling

A Fair Trade Organization

This manifesto is founded on the conviction that one can lead a satisfactory life without having to ruin other people's. The world possesses sufficient resources, if carefully managed and properly distributed, to meet the needs of all of its people, possibly for as long as the species persists. It is only because they are badly managed and poorly distributed that so many human beings are deprived of the means of survival. It is partly because of the profound inequality of outcome caused by this mal-distribution that people correctly perceive themselves to be engaged in a permanent, mortal struggle with other communities. The previous chapters have shown how a greater equality of outcome might arise from an equality of opportunity. This chapter will introduce a more difficult and troubling concept: that in some areas of global governance, the possibility of an equality of outcome can be admitted only by unequal opportunity.

The reason for this is straightforward: nations will enter our new system with wildly different economic positions. Japan's national income averages out at $38,000 per person, Ethiopia's and Burundi's at $100.[103] Were we to devise a system governing the flow of goods and services around the world which offered a perfect equality of opportunity – that is, which permitted equal access for all the world's people – this system would be 380 times better for the people of Japan than it is for the people of Ethiopia.* The world's physical wealth would continue to flow from the poor nations to the rich nations, further impoverishing the poor and enriching the rich. Our 'equitable' system would perpetuate the world's inequality. Fair trade, in other words, requires that the rich nations, like the fastest racehorses, carry a handicap. This chapter proposes a new set of rules for racing.

Trade is the issue which has been of most interest to those members of the global justice movement who live in the rich world. While the *balance* of trade between nations,

---

* This assumes that in the global (as opposed to the national) market-place a dollar has equal purchasing power, whether it is spent by a Japanese person or an Ethiopian. There is considerable controversy surrounding this issue: some theorists would claim that the Ethiopians have a greater relative purchasing power than this example would suggest, others that they have less. The basic point survives, however: that at present the people of the rich nations have a vastly greater power to capture material wealth through world trade than the people of the poor nations.

explored in the last chapter, has been neglected, as its connection to both debt and the depredations of the World Bank and the IMF has not been widely understood, the *rules* governing trade have consistently drawn the biggest crowds onto the streets. I have met people who cannot name their own nation's foreign secretary, but can explain, without blinking, how the World Trade Organization's General Agreement on Trade in Services affects them. For depoliticized people, disenchanted by the lack of choice offered by domestic politics, trade has become the issue which has reawakened their anger. It has, in effect, re-enfranchised them.

There are four reasons for this. The first is a well-founded sense of injustice, built on a recognition of the gross inequalities – of both opportunity and outcome – implicit in the way global trade is regulated. The second, allied to the first concern, is the disquiet about the loss of democratic powers to defend the environment, workers and consumers from corporations. This concern is also well-founded: much of the core business of the global trade regulators is secretive, unaccountable and, as they have often boasted, dispatched in close cooperation with corporate executives. The third reason is anxiety about the erosion of cultural integrity and regional identity. The fourth is the fear of losing jobs to cheaper labour forces overseas. The rich world's coalition against existing trade policies is motivated therefore by a curious mixture of altruism and selfishness. Sometimes these different issues are conflated within a single campaign. The most celebrated of Europe's global justice campaigners, the French farmer Jose Bové, has often been characterized as the continent's leading opponent of free trade. But the immediate motivation for his initial protest – in which he helped to dismantle a McDonald's restaurant – was his anger at the *suspension* of free trade.

The United States had sought, through the World Trade Organization, to force the European Union to import beef from animals reared with the help of growth-promoting hormones. The EU, citing research which suggests that one of these hormones causes cancer in children, had refused to comply. The World Trade Organization permitted the US to impose punitive sanctions on Europe, which it levied, knowing that these would be most keenly felt, on luxury goods. One of the products it selected for a hundred per cent trade tax was Roquefort cheese, which Bové produced. His demolition of the McDonald's was prompted by a number of factors: his disgust at a trade regime which allows some nations to force potentially dangerous products into the markets of others; his distrust of the decision-making process which led to the ruling in favour of the United States; his concern about the erosion of local culture and local cuisine by the ubiquitous McDonald's (whose presence on its soil France was effectively obliged by the trade rules to accept); but above all the loss of the market for his produce in the United States. Jose Bové, in other words, was simultaneously fighting international trade and the cessation of international trade. It is, perhaps, unsurprising that outsiders have occasionally found these campaigns confusing.

Some activists, confronting the gross injustices which govern the way the world's trade rules are set and enforced, and the threats to culture, the environment and states' ability to protect their people from dangerous products or practices, have, as Chapter 3 suggested, argued that most of the trade between nations should be brought to a halt. Trade taxes or 'tariffs', of the kind to which Jose Bové reacted, should be used to prevent foreign producers from competing with domestic producers selling the same products or services. I have come to see that this is the wrong prescription.

Trade, at present, is a feeble, often regressive means of distributing wealth between nations. While a few poor nations have managed to claw back some value, most have received little by way of financial reward for the torrent of material goods which has rushed from their economies into those of the rich world. Some nations appear to have profited from trade only because the damage to their environment has not been costed: had it been, they would surely be seen to have become poorer rather than richer as a result of their exports. Others appear to be making money because the foreign corporations which own their productive capacity are making money, and this money is misleadingly accounted as if it remains within national borders.

But if trade is not the answer, our movement is surely duty-bound to find another. The problem is simply stated. Most of the world's purchasing power resides in the hands of the people who need it least, while those who need it most, for such necessities as food, clean water, housing, health and education, have almost none. If no means is provided of shifting some of that money from those who have more than they need to those who have less than they need, the world will continue to be a miserable place for the majority of its people to inhabit. This redistribution is simply not going to happen through aid. Nations, like people, appear to become more selfish as they get richer. The biggest economy in the world, the United States, offers a smaller proportion of its national wealth in the form of aid than any other substantial donor – a mere 0.1 per cent of its gross domestic product – and this has declined as its economy has grown. Overall, the money given by the rich world to the poor world diminished, in real terms, by $7.1 billion (or twelve per cent) between 1992 and 2000.[104] But even if, in a sudden fit of compassion, the rich world were to start pouring its money freely into the hands of the poor, this would merely trap the poor nations in patronage, dependency and blackmail. Their people would neither respect themselves nor expect to be respected by outsiders.

Besides giving and spending, it is hard to see how money can be extracted from the hands of the rich. Theft has served the powerful nations well, but the poor are in no position

to reciprocate. If giving is destructive of respect and independence, then we are left with nothing but spending. Trade
has, so far, proved an improbable answer to the problems
faced by most nations – but it is the only possible answer.

Indeed, many of those within the global justice movement who explicitly reject trade as a means of distributing
wealth implicitly appear to accept it. They buy fairly traded
coffee and bananas, shop at markets and independent shops
rather than supermarkets and purchase ethnic rugs and
baskets from the development charities. They boycott the
produce of nations whose governments they oppose, knowing that this will hurt them, and encourage people to buy
goods from countries they wish to support.* They could
scarcely fail to be aware, too, of the economic transformation of the lives of some of the people of the developing
world – principally the citizens of some of the countries of
East Asia – and the role that trade played in their nations'
development. The ability of these countries to sell manufactured products at competitive prices has led to a net transfer
of money into their economies, which has helped to raise
hundreds of millions of people from extreme poverty
to comparative prosperity. As the self-respect of workers
in such countries has increased, they have succeeded in
demanding that many of their rights be recognized. In the

---

* There is, for example, a campaign supported by many members of the
  movement to boycott Israeli goods and promote Palestinian produce.

early 1990s, for example, Korean and Taiwanese companies began fleeing to *Britain*, as the workforce there was cheaper and easier to exploit.

The charity Oxfam has shown that, even under the existing unfair system, the poor world obtains thirty-two times as much revenue from exports as it receives from aid.[105] If the poor nations increased their share of world exports by only five per cent, they would reap an extra $350 billion a year, seven times more than they currently obtain from aid. Its simulations suggest that a one per cent increase in the share of world exports for each developing region would reduce the number of people in extreme poverty by 128 million, or twelve per cent of the world's total.[106] The decline would be greatest in those regions suffering the greatest poverty, namely sub-Saharan Africa and South Asia. Poverty can appear to many of the rich world's people as something of an abstraction. It might be easier to understand when we recognize that the immediate cause of famine is not drought or crop failure, but the poorest citizens' lack of purchasing power. As food stocks decline, the price rises, and even if there is, in absolute terms, enough for everyone, the poor have no means of obtaining it. Poverty, for many of the world's people, means death by starvation or one of the diseases associated with it.

If trade is the only likely means of distributing wealth from rich nations to poor ones, it should also be clear that this distribution cannot take place unless there are rules, agreed by all those who participate, which prevent the rich from exploiting the poor. International trade without international rules, as hundreds of years of colonial exploitation show, is piracy. It should also be clear that rules, such as those proposed by some of the opponents of free trade, which permit rich nations to protect their economies against the poor are likely, far from redressing the mal-distribution of global wealth, to exacerbate it. Indeed, it is precisely because of the protectionist devices – some subtle, some crude – which the rich world has deployed that it continues only to remove wealth from many of its poorer partners.

The world's most powerful governments claim that the economic relationship between nations is governed by a single formula, which they call 'free trade'. In reality, there are two formulae. One of them is the market fundamentalism to which the poor nations have been forced to submit. Through the World Trade Organization, the World Bank and the International Monetary Fund, indebted countries have been coerced into opening their markets to foreign corporations and foreign produce, privatizing their services and abandoning the measures which helped small domestic companies to compete with their bigger competitors overseas. The other is the way the rich world lives. The weaker trading nations have been repeatedly promised that every concession they make to free trade will be matched, or more than matched, by similar concessions by the powerful. But while in some respects their market liberalization has exceeded the demands of the World Trade Organization's agreements (largely because of the 'adjustments' engineered by the IMF and World Bank), the rich world has responded by breaking almost every promise it has made.

Across Europe and the United States, farming employs 3.3 per cent of the working population.* In most of the poor world, by contrast, farmers are a majority or a near-majority of the nation's workforce. Fair trade in the products of farming would cost the rich world very little, in terms of the loss of welfare to its inhabitants, while delivering major potential benefits to poorer nations. In 2002, for example, the United States handed $3.9 *billion* dollars (or three times its entire aid budget for Africa) to just 25,000 cotton farmers.[108] This reduced world prices by an estimated twenty-six per cent,[109] destroying the livelihoods of tens of millions of farmers in the poor world. But the meanness of the dominant nations is such that they will permit no other country, if they can prevent it, from outcompeting them in any economic sector, however trivial the domestic impact may be. The poor world possesses what economists call a 'comparative advantage' in most kinds of crop production. Land and labour are cheaper, currencies are weaker and sunlight, in the tropics, is stronger, which

---

* In the US, 3.28 million, or 2.4 per cent of the working population of 135 million are employed in farming or related trades. In the European Union, the figure is 6.63 million, or 4.1 per cent of the workforce of 162 million.[107]

means that plants grow more quickly. This is why the rich world protects its farmers against competition.

Many of the concessions the United States and the European Union have extracted from the poorer nations during trade negotiations have been exchanged for the promise that the subsidies they give their farmers will be scaled down or eliminated. So ruinous are these subsidies to the lives and livelihoods of the people of the poor world that their governments have agreed to almost everything the powerful nations have demanded. They have been rewarded by a flat refusal on the part of the US and Europe to honour the deals. Soon after the latest trade agreement was negotiated, for example, the United States raised the value of farm subsidies by eighty per cent. The rich nations now give their farmers $352 billion a year[110] – or nearly $1 billion a day – which is six and a half times what they give poor nations in the form of aid.

These subsidies permit rich countries to sell crops for less than they cost to produce. There are two devastating consequences for the poor world. The first is that its exports cannot compete with the artificially cheap crops grown by the rich world's farmers. The second is that when the rich world's exports enter the poor world's markets, they undercut the local farmers, forcing them out of business. The poor nations can do little to prevent these cheap goods from flooding their markets, as they have been forced by the rich world to remove both their trade barriers and many of the subsidies they provide for their own farmers.

So ruthless is this distortion of the free market the temperate nations claim to defend that they will seek to outcompete by unfair means even those products in which the tropics specialize. The European Union, for example, spends $1.6 billion a year on subsidizing sugar production, despite the inefficiency of producing sugar from sugarbeet in cool nations by comparison to sugar from sugarcane in hot nations. And where they cannot grow the product at all, they seek to capture most of its value by preventing the producing nations from processing it. The European Union and the US impose 'escalating tariffs' on products such as coffee and chocolate, which means that they let the raw materials enter the country free of charge, but apply higher and higher taxes the more they are processed. As instant coffee is worth far more than green coffee beans, and chocolate far more than fermented cocoa beans, the greater part of the value of production is snatched by the importers.

When the poor nations are unable to process the food they produce, they must export more in order to obtain the same value, which means that they must devote more of their land to cash cropping (and less to producing food for their own people), pay their workers less, clear more tropical forest, drain more marshland, use more pesticides in production and more fossil fuels in transport. The higher the tariff on processed food, the greater the environmental destruction and social dislocation it causes.

Similar restrictions are imposed on manufactured textiles. Here too the poor world has a comparative advantage over most temperate nations, as cotton can be grown locally and labour is cheap. So here too the rich world enforces punishing tariffs. Bangladesh must pay the United States $314 million a year for the privilege of selling its garments in that country.[111] Not only do such impositions discriminate against the poor; they discriminate *specifically* against the poor: rich nations impose, on average, tariffs four times higher on goods from poor nations than on goods from other rich nations, because the other rich nations can fight back. Were trade barriers of this kind to be removed, the poor world would be permitted to export goods worth a further $700 billion a year.[112]

The rich world's blatant protectionism is accompanied by more subtle measures. The World Trade Organization has granted over the years ever more generous global 'intellectual property rights' to corporations.* These have enabled them, for example, to assert exclusive control over genetic material and plant and animal varieties: they can, in some instances, force anyone who wishes to use a plant variety (or even, for certain purposes, a plant species) to pay them a licence fee. This can be seen in the same light as a tariff barrier: it is a form of discriminatory commercial

---

* Through its Agreement on Trade-Related Aspects of Intellectual Property Rights, or TRIPS.

protection. Defenders of this protectionism argue that it applies equally to companies or individuals of all nations, so it is just as likely to be useful to the poor world as it is to the rich. But this is rather like saying that anyone in the United States can buy an apartment in Manhattan. There is no law preventing a US citizen, of any profession or colour or social status, from acquiring one; but only those with plenty of money will be able to do so. Establishing global property rights costs a fortune in legal fees, which means, in practice, that they are available only to the better-financed corporations. All the sectors in which intellectual property is the main determinant of value – the media, information technology, drugs, biotechnology and seed breeding – are dominated by a handful of large companies, nearly all of which are based in the industrialized nations. Ninety-seven per cent of patents are owned by corporations in the rich world.[113] The most recent intellectual property rules will cost poor nations $40 billion a year in licence fees, half of which will be payable to companies based in the United States.[114]

Similar protections are being extended to companies seeking to establish factories or subsidiaries abroad.* The WTO's agreements forbid governments from excluding foreign companies from their countries, or from insisting that, if they do come in, they must use local materials or

---

* By means of the WTO's Trade-Related Investment Measures, or TRIMS.

local labour, invest their profits locally, or export more than they import. Again, this looks like an even-handed measure, but again it greatly favours the industrialized nations. The bigger a corporation becomes, the greater its ability to invest abroad. Of the world's 500 largest companies, only twenty-nine are based in developing countries.[115]

Corporations already enjoy complete 'investor protection' in many countries, with the result that 'foreign direct investment' can sometimes cost a poor nation more money than it makes. Many companies use poor countries as a pool of cheap labour: they import both the machines they need and the components of the products they wish to manufacture and employ local people to assemble or pack them, adding little to their value. They either disguise their profits by buying the components at inflated prices from other subsidiaries of the same company, or simply send their profits back home intact. In Thailand, as the United Nations has shown, foreign direct investment has had a negative net impact on the balance of trade: that is to say, the value of the exports generated by the foreign companies based there is less than the value of their imports combined with the value of the profits they have sent abroad.[116]

There may be good reasons for excluding foreign companies from some sectors of a poor nation's economy. In many cases they do not generate wealth, but merely purchase local companies or displace local production, often with a net loss of jobs for local people. They can prevent

indigenous industries from developing, with serious consequences for the balance of trade. They often wreck fragile
environments, then move away, leaving the nation either
to pay for their restoration or to live with the consequences
of their destruction. Many poor nations have recognized
that their people, their environment and their economies
would be better served by excluding the rich world's companies until they are able to defend themselves, but they
are forced by the international institutions to let them enter.

The rich nations argue that liberalization of this kind is
essential for development: if countries want to make money,
they need to open their economies as much as possible.
This claim is challenged by a remarkable but little-known
truth: that almost every nation which has industrialized successfully and can now be counted as belonging to the
developed world has done so not through free trade but
through protectionism.

The development economist Ha-Joon Chang has spent
the past ten years exposing the founding myth of the industrialized nations.[117] Like all the stories which conquering
powers tell about themselves – of heroism tempered by
compassion, of government in the best interests of the con-
quered – the story of development through free trade and
equal opportunity promulgated by the rich nations is false.
It omits the inconvenient historical detail that free trade
policies were introduced only *after* the industrialized nations
had achieved their economic dominance. During their key

transformative stages, they defended their economies fiercely against competition from other nations.

Britain, for example, regards itself as the patron of free trade. The British believe that they established their industrial revolution and acquired the wealth on which their global empire was built by means of a strict application of the doctrine of *laissez-faire*: permitting businesses to compete freely in a scarcely-regulated market. Nothing could be further from the truth.

Britain's industrial revolution was founded, in its initial stages, upon the textile industry. In the eighteenth century this accounted for over half the nation's export revenues. The industry was nurtured and promoted by means of ruthless government intervention. Textile manufacturing began to develop in the fourteenth century, when Edward III brought Flemish weavers into the country, centralized the trade in raw wool and banned the import of woollen cloth.[118] His successors extended this protectionism. Henry VII, for example, ruined Britain's major competitors – Flanders and Holland – by banning British merchants from exporting raw wool and unfinished cloth. Imports of competing products were not just discouraged through tariffs; in some cases they were prohibited. In 1699, for example, the British state destroyed the Irish woollen industry by forbidding the import of its manufactures, which were of higher quality than English cloth. In 1700, Britain did the same to the Indian producers of calico (cotton cloth), extinguishing the world's most efficient cotton manufacturing industry. Britain also banned steel mills in America, forcing its colony to export only pig iron.

While tariffs on imported raw materials were reduced in the 1720s and 1730s (providing British industry with cheaper inputs), manufactured goods from abroad continued to be heavily taxed. At the same time, the government granted British manufacturers of every processed product from refined sugar to gunpowder generous export subsidies.[119] Only when Britain had established technological superiority in the production of almost all manufactured products did it suddenly discover the virtues of free trade. It was not until the 1850s and 1860s, when it was already the world's dominant economy, that the country opened most of its markets. Even then, the process of liberalization was strictly controlled by the state. Britain's enthusiasm for free trade did not last long. In the early twentieth century, as it began to slip behind the United States and Germany, its manufacturers started lobbying for protectionism, which they were granted during the global Depression in 1932.

The United States, which now insists that no nation can develop without free trade, defended its markets just as aggressively during its key development phase.[120] The first man systematically to set out the case for 'infant industry protection' (defending new industries from foreign competition until they are big enough to compete on equal terms) was Alexander Hamilton, who in 1789 became the first

Secretary of the US Treasury. To help its own manufacturers to develop, the United States introduced progress-
ively higher tariffs. By 1816 the tax on almost all imported
manufactures was thirty-five per cent, rising to forty per
cent in 1820 and, for some goods, fifty per cent in 1832.
Combined with the cost of transporting goods to the US,
this gave domestic manufacturers a formidable advantage
within their home market.

Protectionism was arguably a more immediate cause of
the American Civil War than the abolition of slavery. High
tariffs helped the northern states, which were industrializing
rapidly, but hurt the southern states, which remained
heavily dependent on imports. The Republicans' victory was
the victory of the protectionists over the free traders: in
1864, before the war ended, Abraham Lincoln raised import
taxes to the highest level they had ever reached. The US
remained the most heavily protected nation on earth until
1913.[121] Even then, its liberalization was temporary. In 1922,
tariffs on manufactured imports were re-imposed at thirty
per cent. The infamous Smoot–Hawley Act of 1930, which
exacerbated the Depression, is widely reported as a bizarre
protectionist anomaly, but in reality it was consistent with
140 years of policy. While it introduced trade taxes at forty-
eight per cent, this represented only a minor increase in
protectionism: in 1925, in the middle of what is commonly
described as a period of 'free trade', they stood at thirty-
seven per cent.

Only after World War Two, when its industrial supremacy was unchallenged, did the US drop most of its formal barriers. Even then, it retained several powerful protectionist measures which persist to this day, such as quotas on the import of clothing and textiles, farm subsidies, 'anti-dumping' duties and the demand for 'voluntary export restraints' from other countries, which often turn out to be anything but voluntary. Free trade has arguably never been practised in the United States. Far from suffering as a result of this protectionism, as the US government now insists that poor nations today would suffer, throughout the period in which it remained the most protected nation on earth, it was also the fastest-growing. Indeed, it grew quickest (from 1870–1890 and 1890–1910) when its protectionist barriers were highest.[122]

The market fundamentalists also assert that the growth of the three nations which have developed most spectacularly over the past sixty years – Japan, Taiwan and South Korea – was the result of free trade. Again, they could not be more wrong. All three nations have followed the same basic prescription: land reform, the protection and funding of key industries and the active promotion of exports by the state. They began to allow the import of products which competed with their own only when the domestic industries which produced them had already become world leaders. Indeed, as the last chapter showed, South Korea's economic collapse in 1998 was the direct result of dropping one of its trade barriers: its restrictions on the movement of capital.

All these nations imposed strict controls on foreign companies seeking to establish factories. In South Korea, for example, they were allowed in only if they set up a joint venture with a local firm.[123] In Taiwan they were forced by the tax laws to use local materials and to export more than they imported.[124] They all acquired new technology by ignoring other countries' patents. Their governments invested massively in infrastructure, research and education, and intervened to reorganize companies, closing some down if they felt that domestic competition was impeding the development of export markets. In South Korea and Taiwan, the state owned all the major commercial banks, which permitted it to make the major decisions about investment.[125] In Japan, the Ministry of International Trade and Industry exercised the same control by legal means.[126] They used tariffs and a number of clever legal ruses to shut out foreign products which threatened the development of their new industries.[127] They granted major subsidies for exports. They did, in other words, everything that the World Trade Organization, the World Bank and the IMF forbid or discourage today.

It is not hard to see why the fundamentalists wish to claim the results for themselves. From 1950 to 1973, the Japanese economy grew at an average of eight per cent per capita per year.*[128] Taiwan grew by an average of 6.2 per cent per capita per year throughout the entire period of 1953 to 1986.[129] Between 1965 and 1987, its exports grew a hundred-fold. At the end of the Korean War, South Korea was poorer than Sudan. Its principal export was wigs made of human hair.[130] Between 1963 and 1972, its manufacturing sector grew by 18.3 per cent per year, faster than that of any other developing country since records began. Between 1973 and 1978, it rose to 24.7 per cent.[131] In all three cases, this growth was accompanied by an extraordinary social transformation. Taiwan and South Korea, most of whose people were living at or below the subsistence level sixty years ago, now have some of the best health, welfare and education figures on earth: Taiwan, for example, has almost one hundred per cent literacy, very nearly full employment, a national income per head higher than New Zealand's and a life expectancy (seventy-five years) just a little behind that of the United States.[132] Taiwan and Japan are among the nations with the world's best distribution of wealth.

There is also no shortage of evidence to suggest that the nations which remain poor today have encountered greater economic success during those periods in which their governments intervened more actively in their economies. Several studies have contrasted the rates of growth in the poor nations between 1960 and 1980, when most of them

---

* The per capita rate takes population growth into account.

protected and promoted their infant industries, with their rates of growth between 1980 and 2000 when they were forced (largely by the IMF) to stop such interventions. One survey of 116 nations suggests that national income per head grew by 3.1 per cent per year between 1960–1980, but just 1.4 per cent between 1980 and 2000.[133] The poorest nations were the hardest hit: growth in sub-Saharan Africa fell from thirty-six per cent across the first twenty years to *minus* fifteen per cent between 1980 and 1998. Another study suggests that Latin America's growth fell from seventy-three per cent in the first period to six per cent in the second, and Africa's from thirty-four per cent to minus twenty-three per cent.[134] Partly as a result, the number of people in sub-Saharan Africa living on less than $1 a day rose, according to UN figures, from 242 million to 300 million between 1990 and 1999.*[135]

Yet another set of figures suggests that the share of global trade taken by the world's forty-nine poorest nations has halved since 1980.[136] This is likely to drop still further: in 1997 the UNDP calculated that sub-Saharan Africa would be $1.2 billion poorer as a result of the latest world trade agreement.[137]

---

* This actually represents a small percentage decline (from 47.7 to 46.7 per cent), however, as Africa's population has grown in that period. An absolute growth in the numbers in extreme poverty is nonetheless shocking, and the converse of the predictions made by the international institutions.

Of course, it does not follow from all this that protectionism in poor nations is always beneficial. In many countries it has been deployed as a means of defending the uncompetitive and exploitative industries run by the president's family or friends, at great cost to both consumers and the wider economy. But what we can conclude is that, on many occasions in history, it has been used to devastating effect in propelling a nation through its key phase of development.

The trade policies forced upon the poor world by the rich world today are consistent with the inequitable rules the imperial powers imposed in the past. Throughout the nineteenth century, Britain used its military and economic power to force 'unequal treaties' upon weaker nations, such as Brazil (1810), Siam (1824), Persia (1836 and 1837), the Ottoman Empire (1838 and 1861), China (1842) and Japan (1858). Just as the IMF forces the poor nations, but not the rich, to drop their trade barriers, Britain forbade all these nations from imposing any but the most minimal tariffs, but refused to accept corresponding obligations. None of these nations were able to start industrializing until they shook off these treaties and introduced effective protection for their own infant industries.

The poor nations continue to be forced to apply precisely the opposite formula for development to that pursued by almost all the countries which are rich today. Far from imposing free trade as a means of helping poor nations to develop, the continuity between today's policies and the unequal treaties of the past suggests that the rich countries are instead engaged in a deliberate policy of forcing the poor world to remain both a cheap source of labour and raw materials and an open market for their manufactured goods and services. Indeed, if these policies were good for the poor nations, it is hard to see why the rich nations would have had to impose them.

The curious aspect of this story is that the World Trade Organization, which sets and enforces the rules under which nations trade, is in principle the most democratic of all the powerful international institutions. Every nation which belongs to it has one vote, and unpopular measures can, in theory, be blocked by a constitutional minority of its members. If the poor nations feel they are being treated unfairly, they can bring negotiations to a halt, just as they did, spectacularly, during the world trade talks in Seattle in 1999. As there are many more poor nations than rich ones, we could expect the poor regularly to outvote the rich. But, like all the other mechanisms of global governance, the trade organization has been captured. Most of the weak nations have an opportunity to vote only *after* the key decisions have been taken.

Before a new round of trade talks begins, the agenda is first established by a group of nations called 'the Quad': the United States, the European Union, Canada and Japan. They and a small number of poorer countries – a different assortment every time – conduct a number of 'Green Room' meetings, during which all the principal business of the new trade round is decided. The Green Room, in other words, is the WTO's Security Council, and the Quad is its permanent membership. The WTO is as exclusive, in practice, as the United Nations. Those other countries which are permitted by the Quad to attend the Green Room negotiations are treated by the more powerful players just as the temporary members of the UN Security Council are treated by the residents. During the last trade round, an African delegate complained that 'If I speak out too strongly, the US will phone my minister. They will twist the story and say that I am embarrassing the United States. My government will not even ask, "What did he say?" They will just send me a ticket tomorrow ... I fear that bilateral pressure will get me, so I don't speak, for fear of upsetting the master. To me, that threat is real. Because I am from a poor country, I can't say what I want.'[138] If the poor nations complain, the rich nations simply withdraw their aid or freeze their exports.

By the time the formal, constitutional trade talks are ready to begin, the key decisions have already been made. An agenda has been set and a declaration has been drafted, and all the nations which were excluded from the Green Room meetings can do is seek to block the rich nations' proposals. They cannot make proposals of their own; they cannot set a new agenda. They are presented with a stark choice: either they accept the declaration drafted in their absence, more or less in its entirety, or they reject it. At Seattle, they decided to reject it, and the trade talks collapsed. But this left them without the means of meeting their needs for fairer treatment, of persuading the rich countries to drop their punishing farm subsidies and their escalating tariffs on processed goods. In Qatar two years later, when the talks recommenced, the excluded nations accepted most of the contents of the declaration drafted in the Green Room meetings, in the hope of gaining some remission from the grotesque distortions of the 'free trade' regime. As the rich world has already broken most of the promises it made in Qatar, this may be the last trade agreement the poor world is prepared to sign.

Perhaps we should see the gulf between the constitution and the practice of the World Trade Organization as a ghastly warning for the alternative institutions we seek to establish. In principle, the WTO grants the governments of the poor world more collective decision-making power than the governments of the rich world. In practice, it has permitted the realities of power to reassert themselves. The strong states have devised a means of bypassing collective decision-making, while the weak states have proved reluctant to use their constitutional powers to stop them, for fear of punishment. They may grumble, but ultimately they will do what they are told, as the savage consequences of defying the Quad outweigh the savage consequences of obeying it. Our systems will need to be robust, transparent, accountable and subject to constant public scrutiny. Those who live in the rich world must never cease to hold their governments to account. Those who live in the poor need entertain no doubts that unless they act in concert they may as well not act at all.

It should surely be obvious, therefore, that any measures which permit the rich world further to protect its economies against the poor will contribute to injustice and impede the distribution of wealth. It should be a matter of concern to everyone within the global justice movement that, in the rich world, our most audible response so far to the injustices of global trade has been to call for universal protectionism. Localization insists that nothing which can be produced locally should be imported. It thus excludes the poor from the rich world's market, which, by definition, is where the money is. While there is a case for permitting *poor* nations to protect some parts of their economies, the localization proposals which permit rich nations to do the same are inherently regressive.

Both free trade and localization effectively condemn many poor nations to remain trapped in the role of purveyors of cheap commodities to the rich world. Free trade does so because an infant industry – an industry which is starting to develop a range of products or services in a nation for the first time – is unlikely to be able to survive in direct conflict with established competitors overseas. The competitors have experience, intellectual property rights, established marketing networks and economies of scale* on their side; the infant industries have none of these advantages. Developing in direct competition with established industries, therefore, is like learning to swim in a torrent: you are likely to be swept away and drowned long before you acquire the necessary expertise.

This is the science applied by all but three of the rich nations which established their wealth independently.† Only Switzerland, Holland and Belgium appear to have developed their industrial base without the use of major infant industry protection policies, and in all cases they were able to do so, as Chang points out, only because they possessed certain material advantages (such as the Netherlands' naval power) and were already close – both scientifically and geographically – to the world's technological frontier.[139] The wealth gap between their citizens and those of the technological leaders, measured in terms of what economists call 'purchasing power parity' was insignificant; today, by contrast, the citizens of the poorest nations have adjusted incomes ninety-five times lower than those of the richest nations.[140] Switzerland and Holland, by abandoning intellectual property protection during their key development

---

* Economies of scale means that it is cheaper to produce an item if it is one of a million than if it is one of a hundred.
† Rather than through redistribution within the European Union.

phases, also freely stole the technologies of the more industrialized nations, granting themselves the 'technology transfer' now forbidden to poor countries by the WTO's patents
regime.[141]

Localization, on the other hand, effectively forbids the
poor nations' infant industries to grow up. In one respect,
the policy appears to make some sense. Perhaps the gravest
problem the world now confronts is climate change, and
the sector whose contribution to climate change is growing
most rapidly is transport. The movement of goods around
the world is extraordinarily wasteful and inefficient: grain
is shipped from one side of the world to the other, passing
freighters which are transporting an identical cargo in the
opposite direction. Salad vegetables, grown with water
stolen from the Samburu people, and with the help of pesticides which are wrecking the ecology of the savannahs, are
flown from Kenya to Britain in planes which are helping to
heat the planet, on night flights which wreck the sleep of
the people who live on the flight paths, while hundreds of
acres of British greenhouses fall into dereliction.

This is reverse ergonomics, the most destructive and
illogical of all possible means of bringing goods to the
market. It prevails for several reasons. One is that, as we
have seen, poor nations are forced to export vast quantities
of bulky items to make the money required to pay their
debts, because the rich world won't permit them to export
smaller, more valuable products. Another is that, because

poor nations are not permitted to control the value of goods imported by the foreign corporations which use them as sources of cheap labour, vast quantities of components are shipped from one assembly plant to another, sometimes on different sides of the world, with minor additions to the product made in each factory. But the overriding reason is that the cost of items such as environmental damage and the theft of other people's resources are not included in the price of the product. These costs have been 'externalized', which is another way of saying that other people (in the case of the Kenyan vegetables, the Samburu and all those who will one day suffer as a result of climate change) pick up the bill.

This profound injustice must be tackled, and later in this chapter I will suggest the means by which this might happen. But dealing with climate change by imposing – as some of the most prominent localizers suggest – punitive tariffs on any items which could be produced at home is like insisting that an entire town be imprisoned because one of its citizens has poisoned the water supply: not only is the measure insufficiently targeted, but it ensures that those who are suffering already as a result of the crime are forced to suffer even more.

A similar argument applies to the exploitation of workers by companies producing goods for export. It is true that workers, particularly women, are treated abysmally in export processing zones all over the poor world. They suffer from poor wages, long hours, exposure to toxins and industrial injuries and sexual abuse. Trades unions are banned in many of these zones and there is no maternity leave or security of employment. But while our movement has rightly emphasized the contrast between the poverty of the workers and the wealth of the corporations which are exploiting them, the aggressive optimism of the adverts for the products they make and the misery of those who make them, we appear to have failed to show that workers supplying the domestic market in the same nations are treated any better. Indeed, there is plenty of evidence to suggest that, whether they are employed as paid or debt-bonded farm labourers, stone-breakers, charcoal-stokers or servants for local aristocrats, the workers employed in domestic enterprises are treated just as badly; in many cases even worse. This is one of the reasons why, despite the dreadful conditions in many export processing zones, there appears to be no shortage of applicants for jobs there.* What this suggests is that trade itself is not the problem: the problem lies with the way workers of all kinds are treated in some nations. Later in the chapter I will also suggest how we might address this issue.

---

* Another important reason, often neglected, is the lack of access to land: workers in many of the export zones are exploitable as they are almost infinitely replaceable, as a result of the vast numbers driven off the land. Land reform is an essential prerequisite for labour rights.

Localization, as Colin Hines explains it, insists that all countries should 'produce as much of their food, goods and services as they can. Anything that can't be provided nationally should be obtained regionally, with long-distance trade the very last resort ... Some long-distance trade will still occur for those sectors providing goods and services to other regions of the world that can't provide such items from within their own borders, e.g. certain minerals or cash crops.'[142] To earn foreign exchange from the rich world, in other words, the poor world must export raw materials.

If the history of trade teaches us one lesson it is that the production of raw materials for export rewards only those who succeed in monopolizing the primary resource. Oil is a partial exception, as the volume and value of production in some states in the Middle East has been so stupendous that, hard as the ruling class has tried to sequester the entire benefit for itself, some wealth has oozed from between its fingers. But even deposits of gold appear to have impoverished rather than enriched the people of most of the nations which possess them, binding them into exploitative relationships first with the pirate fleets of other nations, then with the pirate corporations.

The only economy on earth which has grown more swiftly than those of East Asia over the past thirty years is Botswana's. Almost all its growth was the result of the extraction of a single raw material, albeit a rather valuable one: diamonds. While the economies of Japan, Taiwan and South Korea, whose wealth arose from manufacturing, are among the most egalitarian on earth, Botswana's, by the early 1990s, was one of the most unequal: the richest twenty per cent of the population earned more than twenty-five times as much as the poorest twenty per cent.[143] While Taiwan has almost full employment, Botswana, at twenty-two per cent, has the world's sixth highest unemployment rate. Today, while Japan has the highest life expectancy (eighty-one years), Botswana has the world's lowest (thirty-six years).[144] One of the few products of Botswana's increased economic activity which has been widely shared by its poorer inhabitants is AIDS. Women driven into prostitution by poverty are purchased by the truck drivers delivering goods to the elite.

Once a company, an individual or a corrupt governing class has asserted ownership of a primary resource, it has little difficulty in ensuring that most of the fruits of production accrue to itself. Almost all the labour required to extract the commodity is unskilled, so wages remain low. There is no need to educate the workers, so there is less danger that they become empowered and politically effective. Every worker without specialized skills is replaceable by any other, so there is no requirement for the owners of plantations or mines to accede to demands for union recognition, decent wages, overtime payments, maternity leave, pensions, social security or healthcare.

Those who seek to become wealthy by means of specialized manufacturing, by contrast, are forced to distribute some of the wealth they accrue to their workforce. Labour is able to demand better wages and better conditions as it becomes more specialized, more expensive to train and harder to replace. Governments which are forced to educate their people by the demands of their manufacturers are likely to discover that those people are harder to oppress.

The extent to which economies are built upon either manufacturing or primary production also affects the distribution of wealth between *nations*. A cup of coffee in the rich world may cost us $3, but the farmer who produced the component which makes it worth drinking received between two and three cents. With the exception of those derived from the most valuable commodities (such as diamonds), the greater part of the cost of the finished product has always been secured not by the people who produce it but by the people who refine, process, manufacture, package and distribute it. While localization might permit nations to rise to the second stage of economic development – processing and selling the products, such as coffee and cocoa, which the rich world cannot produce itself – it forbids them, by the imposition of tariffs,* to start exporting more complex and valuable manufactures, such as computers or

---

* Colin Hines describes tariffs as the instrument 'of most use in the transition from globalization to localization'.[145]

televisions, as these could also be produced in the rich world. Their economies would shift, at best, from stone-breaking to sweatshops; but they could not move beyond that point.

Localization would, moreover, paradoxically damage precisely those interests it seeks to protect. To earn sufficient foreign exchange to import the goods they cannot produce themselves, the poor nations would (as this system forbids them to earn it by any other means) need to export more, not less, of their natural wealth, thus increasing their contribution to climate change, soil erosion and the loss of biodiversity. The more commodities they export, the more the price will fall, which means that they must then export a still greater volume in order to earn the same amount of foreign exchange. While the market fundamentalists' claim that a nation cannot protect the environment until it becomes rich is nonsense (indeed the richest nations are those which do most damage to the environment), it is surely true to say that a nation cannot protect its ecosystem if its economic growth is reliant upon biological growth, as the demand for foreign exchange will soon outstrip the ecosystem's rate of renewal.

A continued reliance on agricultural exports is also likely to accelerate the destruction of the economic sector the localizers are keenest to preserve – smallholder farming. As international trade rewards, to a greater extent than local sales, economies of scale, an export economy based on farming tends to encourage the displacement of small farmers by large ones. The unemployment this causes drives down the cost of labour, ensuring that those who work in the crop-processing industries are exposed to even crueller terms of employment.

The localizers insist that there would be nothing to stop such nations from developing manufactured products for their own markets. Indeed, 'import substitution' is a strategy which has benefited some poor nations. But many countries are so poor that they do not possess a domestic market of sufficient size to make high-value manufacturing worth-while. Even if they do, they are still left with the problem we have just encountered. To produce most of the manufac-tured goods they need for their own consumption, they would have to import the necessary materials and com-ponents, which means that they must acquire foreign exchange, which requires that they must export raw materials. The poor world, in this system, remains trapped in both the agricultural economy and – as a result – in its subordinate relationship to the rich world. Localization is a further imposition upon the lives of the powerless by the people of the powerful nations. It belongs to the age from which we are seeking to escape: the Age of Coercion.

By determining what unfair trade looks like, we can begin to see what the preconditions for fair trade may be. A fair trading system is one which permits poorer nations, and poorer people within those nations, to deploy such measures as are necessary to escape from the poverty trap and, eventually, compete on equal terms with the rich. This surely requires that they should be allowed, when this is necessary, to deploy the strategy which has permitted almost all the world's rich nations to develop, namely infant industry protection. Until a nation reaches a certain level of wealth or development, it should be permitted to defend certain industries with the help of tariff barriers, other import restrictions and development and export subsidies. It should be able to impose strict conditions upon foreign investors: companies can enter the country only if they are prepared to leave behind more wealth than they extract. It should be permitted, in certain circumstances, to override intellectual property protections, to grant itself the technology transfer now denied by the trade rules to most impoverished nations. Rich nations, on the other hand, would be required to pull down their barriers to trade. They would be permitted neither to subsidize their industries nor to impose tariffs or other restraints upon imports from poorer nations.

This appears discriminatory, but it is in fact perfectly even-handed, as nations would be forced gradually to lift their protections as they develop. As those nations which are poor today became rich, they would be obliged to start to liberalize their economies to the same degree as the countries with which they had caught up. At every stage of development they would be required to reduce their protections and shed some of their privileges. This system, by establishing a gradient of opportunity, permits an equality of outcome forestalled by both free trade and localization.

- But while this system depends upon the protectionism deployed by the poor, it should slowly push the world towards free trade. There are several reasons why this is a desirable outcome. Protectionism can create a commodious habitat for corruption, as industrial lobby groups seek to persuade their governments that they require greater subsidies and export privileges than other sectors. It can shelter destructive and wasteful practices, and it raises the price of essential goods for consumers. These dangers can be partly offset by transparency and regulation, but they are likely to re-emerge repeatedly. Perhaps most importantly, when nations achieve a roughly similar economic status, free trade is likely to be the most equitable means of governing their relationship with each other.

But it should be clear that temporary protectionism as a means to development would accelerate the redistribution of wealth between nations. This policy also reduces the need to attract foreign investment in order to stimulate domestic industry. Foreign companies have been deemed necessary to a nation's development only because, unlike the country's own infant industries, they can compete successfully with other transnational firms, and because intellectual property rights have ensured that the only way to acquire certain technologies is to import the companies which control them. If poor nations are permitted, through protectionism and technology transfer, to develop their own competitive industries, they abandon the need to open their doors to companies which insist on repatriating their profits, importing more than they export and demanding lower labour and environmental standards. If nations do not need to attract foreign corporations, they can close the 'export processing zones' in which unions are banned, pollution controls are abandoned and foreigners need pay no taxes.

There is no single formula for economic development. Some nations might discover that their needs are, in fact, best served by opening their borders. Others may find that while technology transfer is important, tariff barriers are not, or that the costs of export subsidies outweigh the benefits they deliver. We must strive not to do as the market fundamentalists and the localizers have done: namely to impose a single, coercive system upon everyone, or, more accurately, upon the poor nations. Instead, our system should provide those countries with the opportunity to use whatever tools they require for their development. If they don't wish to use them, that is up to them.

There has been a great deal of talk within the global justice movement of the need to compensate the poor world for centuries of colonial plunder, slavery and environmental destruction. But some of the proposals raised appear paternalistic: the rich world should 'forgive' the debts of the poor world, or should raise significantly the aid it provides. What better compensation could there be than to permit the poor world to pursue its own path to development, if necessary at the expense of the rich world, without reliance upon the generosity or goodwill of its former colonial masters?

I have been arguing so far as if from a position of adversity, as if, in other words, these proposals were so outrageous and outlandish that no powerful nation could ever accept them, even in theory. In fact, the intellectual case for permitting the poor nations – but only the poor nations – to protect parts of their economies was accepted long ago. The original postwar proposal for regulating trade between nations – the International Trade Organization – provided, in the words of its chief US negotiator, Clair Wilcox, for 'each of the less developed countries [to] make its own decisions as to the industries it wishes to promote. Where public assistance is required, it will be free to subsidize new industries.'[146] It also envisaged measures for transferring technology to poorer nations and for preventing companies from forming global monopolies or from aggressively extending the use of their patents. Though the organization was defended by President Truman, it was blocked by the US Congress, partly as a result of vigorous corporate lobbying.*

---

* The ITO was a US proposal, whose development began in 1943. Its charter was drafted in Havana in 1948. Truman was determined to produce a treaty which would be acceptable to most countries, partly in order to prevent a repetition of the tariff war of the 1930s. The US quietly dropped the proposal in 1950, after Congress kept delaying its

Both the United Nations General Assembly and the UN Conference on Trade and Development have published reports calling for the protection of infant industries. The World Bank, before it was completely captured by the market fundamentalists, used to advise developing countries to engage in 'import substitution'.*[148] Even the WTO provides for the 'special and differential treatment' of poorer countries, though this provision has now become all but useless. In reality, trade barriers are being removed so swiftly in the poor nations by the IMF, the World Bank and the WTO, and erected or sustained so effectively in the rich nations, that the only countries which could now be said to enjoy special and differential treatment are the members of the Quad. The principle of permitting poorer nations to protect some parts of their economies has been rejected not because it doesn't work, but because it does.

Even if, by the means proposed below, we were to succeed in implementing a system which permitted the redistribution of wealth between nations, our scheme still leaves several of the crucial problems which exercise the global

---

consideration. Congress had been lobbied by both corporate free traders (who saw it as too protectionist) and corporate protectionists (who saw it as too liberal).[147]

* Reducing imports by producing the same goods at home.

justice movement either unsolved or only incidentally addressed. The most obvious of these are poor labour standards, environmental destruction and the inordinate power of the corporations.

International trade is, at present, characterized by several ugly and unpleasant features. It has, as we have seen, led to destructive competition between nations seeking foreign investment. Corporations wishing to invest abroad seek the cheapest of all possible conditions: low wages; no obligation to pay for pensions, health insurance or other benefits; low health and safety and environmental standards; low tax; and few regulations to prevent them from extracting as much money from the nation as they can, while leaving behind whatever mess they choose to make. Through a combination of their own financial muscle and the political power of the nations from which they come, these companies have often been able to override the democratic will of the people in whose nations they invest. International transport is contributing massively to climate change, while extractive industries have destroyed entire ecosystems and displaced peasant farmers and the indigenous population. It is not hard to see why some people, mistaking the symptoms for the causes and the causes for the symptoms, have called for the cessation of most forms of international trade.

Those of us within the global justice movement who have called for fair trade rather than no trade, however, have also made a mistake. In seeking to address the need for labour rights, environmental protection and the restraint of corporations, we have tended to separate these issues. The corporations must be restricted, we have argued, but the bodies responsible for preventing the destruction of the environment and the downward pressure on labour rights should be the nation states. Many campaigners in the rich world have suggested that the best way to arrest the race to the bottom is to discriminate, through tariffs or other measures, against imports emanating from countries with poor environmental or labour standards.

While there is no question that many of the poor world's governments represent their people poorly, if at all, and evince little concern for the treatment of their workers or the damage to the environment, and therefore the living conditions of their citizens, it seems to me that trade measures are the wrong means of seeking to change their policies. The tariffs some campaigners have proposed have been perceived by many of the people of poorer nations as yet another means of discriminating against their exports. There may be some truth in this, as some of those who have most eagerly pursued them have been the trades unions in rich countries who fear that their members' jobs are threatened by cheaper labour overseas. A report published in 2001 by the American union the AFL-CIO, for example, called for 'closer economic ties with the rest of the world unless it damages our workers'. It suggested that goods produced in countries whose governments maintained low labour standards should 'be subject to such trade restrictions as tariffs or import bans'.[149] The unfortunate result has been to pitch some of the labour movements of the rich world against the labour movements of the poor world.

Moreover, if labour standards were to be maintained through pressure on nations brokered by the WTO, countries would be forced to comply by means of its complaints and arbitration procedures, which tend, as they are so expensive, to favour the rich world. The poor nations, as a result of the rich world's complaints, justified or otherwise, that their products were unfairly cheap because their labour and environmental standards were too low, could become tangled up in so many cripplingly expensive legal processes that it would no longer be worth their while to export. There is also the danger that this permits the rich world, as ever, to dictate the national policies of the poor world. A universal ban on child labour, for example, which could be the effective result of punitive measures against poorer nations, would be deeply resented by many families which are so poor that they have no option but to send their children to work. We are, yet again, pre-empting any decisions the people of those nations might make, and punishing them if they make what we believe are the wrong ones. We are imposing blanket conditions which take no account of the differences *between* the poor nations and the legitimate conflicts of interest *within* them. Unsurprisingly, such demands from the rich world are deeply resented by the very people they are supposed to help: the workers of the poor world.

The state, like a tree, is essentially immobile. While it can expand its access to resources by extending its roots into the soil on which other trees are growing, it must adapt to the circumstances in which it finds itself. The corporations, like omnivorous animals, are mobile. They move from tree to tree, taking shelter in the branches, preying upon both the trees which protect them and the other members of the ecosystem, seeking always the most easily-obtained resources. The burden of predation has now become so great that most of the trees in the wood appear to be suffering from what foresters call 'die-back'.

As a movement, we have long recognized this relationship. We have repeatedly complained that the corporations are overwhelming the resistance of the state, and that the state, being immobile and reactive, is poorly placed to strike back. We know that some of the corporations have become so fat by feeding upon the other members of the ecosystem that their sheer weight is beginning to snap some of the branches of the state. So it seems curious to me that some of us persist in suggesting that it is the state, not the corporation, which requires international regulation. We should surely regulate first those organisms which have the most agency, and we should regulate *internationally* those actors which move between nations.

Throughout this manifesto, I have sought to suggest ways in which we can use the strengths of our opponents to our advantage, and it seems to me that the roaming hunger of the corporations is another asset we can turn to our account. We know that they move from nation to nation, seeking ever-lower standards. We must force them instead to seek ever-higher ones. If we oblige corporations to set high standards, by punishing them for the destruction, oppression or dispossession caused by the trade in which they engage, then the market begins to work for the poor. We do not apply blanket restrictions upon the way a nation regulates its employers, but we create a major incentive for good practice. The people of the poor nations, who are perfectly capable of deciding what is in their own best interests, can pursue the case for changes in national legislation themselves, aided by the contrast the new global trade rules establish between the standards the export industry has to set and the standards fixed by the domestic employers. But instead of constantly eroding national standards by threatening to move elsewhere unless countries offer them more lenient terms, the corporations, in this system, encourage their elevation.

So the first function of what we might call a Fair Trade Organization is surely to prescribe and enforce the standards to which corporations wishing to trade internationally must conform. It could, in this respect, function as a licensing body: a company would not be permitted to trade between nations unless it could demonstrate that, at every stage of production, manufacture and distribution, its own operations and those of its suppliers and subcontractors met the specified standards.

If, for example, a food-processing company based in Switzerland wished to import cocoa from Côte d'Ivoire, it would need to demonstrate to the Fair Trade Organization that the plantations it bought from were not employing slaves, using banned pesticides, expanding into protected tropical forests, or failing to conform to whatever other standards the organization set. Its performance would be assessed, at its own expense, by a monitoring company accredited to the organization. There is, in other words, no difference between this process and that which prevails within the voluntary fair trade movement today: an agency sets the standards, a company applies for certification, a monitoring company is employed to discover whether or not it qualifies, and if it does so it is permitted to trade. In this case, however, fair trade is no longer voluntary, and no longer depends on the whimsical attentions of the consumer. It is both mandatory and universal.

So we do not need to question whether this works: it works already, for thousands of operations involving the production of food, drinks, timber, clothing, furniture and cosmetics. The problem is simply that, for the reasons outlined in Chapter 3, fair trade currently accounts for a minuscule proportion of the produce bought and sold between nations.

Nor do we need to devise an entire set of new regulations. Since 1919, the International Labour Organization has been developing standards by which we can judge the fair treatment of workers, and has produced a comprehensive set of 'Principles Concerning Multinational Enterprises'.[150] The United Nations Commission on Human Rights has drafted a collection of 'guidelines for companies'.[151] The Organization for Economic Cooperation and Development has developed similar standards.[152] The problem is that, unless they are enforced by individual nation states, all these noble objectives remain voluntary. It should be possible by now to see that voluntary regulations are completely useless, and that those who continue to advocate them, and the accompanying extension of 'consumer democracy' necessary to implement them, are either avoiding trouble or being paid by the companies which hope to prevent change. While there are no compulsory and comprehensive global regulations to constrain corporations' behaviour, they can force governments to abandon their national laws, by threatening to disinvest. A mandatory set of international regulations, by contrast, finds them wherever they are.

Nor do we need to start from scratch when devising a means of enforcing these rules. In most nations, health and safety inspectors must approve an industrial premises before it is permitted to operate. If the company's procedures are found to be unsafe, it is put on notice: it must take immediate steps to change them, or cease operating. If it breaks the rules, it can be fined; if, in some countries, it breaks them persistently or exposes its staff, its neighbours or its customers to a grave risk, it can lose its licence to trade and its directors can face prosecution. We merely need to apply that well-established national principle at the international level. To prosecute company directors, we could seek to expand the mandate of the International Criminal Court. No longer would governments such as India's be left impotently to wave writs which will never be served upon such people as the chief executive of the Union Carbide corporation, who can avoid arrest and prosecution on charges of culpable homicide following the catastrophe at Bhopal simply by staying away from India. If corporations operate internationally so, surely, should the rules. By restraining the corporations, we prevent them from restricting the democratic choices of the countries in which they operate.

There are, however, a few standards we might wish to add to the list. One of the prerequisites of justice, for example, is that producers and consumers should carry their own costs, rather than dumping them on other people. Those who do the dumping tend to be the rich and powerful, while those who are dumped upon tend to be the weak and indigent. Environmental and social 'externalities', in other words, typically represent the theft by the wealthy of the natural and material wealth possessed by the poor. They amount to a monumental subsidy for the rich. It is a source of constant astonishment to me that those who profess to support free market economics routinely overlook this distortion.

This theft has reached so great a scale that it is arguable that the majority of the world's large corporations depend on it for their continued existence. The American professor of business administration Ralph Estes found that if one took into account only those costs which had been properly established by authoritative studies, in 1994 corporations in the United States were permitted to inflict $2.6 trillion-worth of social and environmental damage, or five times the value of their total profits.[153] Many companies object that if they were forced to pay the full price for the resources they use and the damage they cause, they would be driven out of business. To this the only sensible answer is 'good'. Wealth, in this case, would cease to be stolen from the poor and handed to the rich. The price of the most damaging goods would rise enormously, but this should surely please the practitioners of free trade, as it provides a classic 'market response' to a social and environmental problem. Unlike localization, it punishes only those who cause the damage, and offers relative rewards to those who export less harmful goods.

If natural resources were valued according to the cost of their loss to other people, the trade in salad vegetables from the Samburu's land in Kenya would immediately become prohibitively expensive, as the water stolen from them is invaluable, and the damage inflicted upon the climate by the necessary airfreight is out of proportion to any value delivered to consumers in Britain. The monitoring firms deployed by the Fair Trade Organization would determine whether or not companies are paying a fair price for the resources they use. To qualify for a licence to trade, they would, among other costs, have to buy enough of a nation's carbon quota to cover the fossil fuel they or their suppliers consume.*

One of the many beneficial impacts of full-cost accounting is that everything which *can* be processed in the country of origin *will* be processed in the country of origin. No company would seek to export raw logs, bauxite, coffee beans or cotton, as these require far more energy to transport from one place to another than the finished products, such as furniture, aluminium pans, instant coffee and T-shirts, currently manufactured on the other side of the world. Those nations which are, at present, locked into the export of raw materials will suddenly discover that they become the most favoured locations for manufacturing. This proposal, then, precisely inverts the formula championed

---

* This assumes that, as the 'contraction and convergence' model recommends, every nation has been allocated, on the basis of its population, a certain allowance of greenhouse gas production. Nations can choose to sell their surplus quota to other countries or to corporations.

by the localizers, which discourages the export of everything *except* primary produce.

This does not mean that governments are relieved of all responsibilities. We can anticipate that our system would stimulate a lively black market in unmonitored goods. Like the states which have signed the Montreal protocol on ozone-depleting chemicals or the Convention on International Trade in Endangered Species, all governments which belong to the Fair Trade Organization would be obliged to seek to restrict this trade. Enforcement will never be watertight, but those nations – the rich ones – which import most will be those best equipped to regulate the trade.

A Fair Trade Organization would seek to implement, internationally, yet another well-established national principle: that no company should be permitted to dominate the market. While all developed economies try to prevent companies from capturing more than a certain proportion of any economic sector, at the global level there are no such restraints, with the result that the international trade in commodities in particular is dominated by a handful of companies, many of which routinely abuse their position to drive down the prices they pay their suppliers while maintaining the prices they charge their customers. Again, we need not innovate; we need merely apply the rules designed to prevent the establishment of national monopolies to international trade.

Our Fair Trade Organization also permits us to prevent corporations from devolving their liabilities to their subsidiaries. Typically, companies involved in hazardous operations overseas operate through offshoots, often trading under a different name. As soon as they encounter trouble – when, for example, they are sued by the workers they have exposed to asbestos, or are instructed by a government to clean up the pollution they have caused – they withdraw the subsidiary's assets. It goes bankrupt, leaving the dying workers without compensation and the government to mop up the mess it made. Companies which are regulated internationally can no longer flee from the rules. Our Fair Trade Organization should be able to pursue them and their assets all over the world. Corporations will become accountable for every crime they commission.

By such means, corporations are slowly turned into our slaves. Instead of driving down standards, they are forced to raise them. Instead of draining wealth from the poor, they are forced to return it. Many, perhaps most, will go under in the attempt, and we should delight to see them drown. Those which will survive are the companies which, like the fair trade companies today, deliver benefits commensurate with those they receive. By these means, in other words, we can transform the ethics of global trade: only the nice guys survive.

It may seem strange for an anti-corporate campaigner to suggest that corporations can become part of the solution.

But, in principle, a corporation is simply a means of exchanging goods and services for money, a vehicle which carries wealth to and from the bank. They have threatened democracy, damaged the environment, abused their workers and poisoned their neighbours because we have permitted them to do so. We must reduce them to the creatures they are supposed to be: machines, which like cars or computers or dishwashers, have no rights, no privileges, no powers. But it seems to me that we could ban them altogether only if we were prepared to contemplate either a world without global trade or a command economy, neither of which, for the reasons outlined in this book, is an attractive prospect. Even the smallest fair traders operate through companies, and few people within our movement would deny that these firms have delivered benefits to the people with whom they work. But we must never forget that the corporation is a dangerous entity, a machine which is ever ready to spring into life, the engine which begins to walk. We must retain the ability to switch it off whenever it begins to claim the rights and privileges of a human being.

Export growth, then, comes under our system to measure something quite different. At present it represents a mixture of gains and losses to national well-being, misleadingly compounded into a single figure. The loss of natural resources is added to the genuine addition of value provided by the application of labour. Our prescription effectively separates these measures. The extraction and export of natural resources will in most cases be accounted as a loss to the national economy. The application of human labour and the deployment of skill will be measured as a gain. Nations will be able to see immediately whether they are being enriched or impoverished through trade.

This does not, of course, solve all the world's environmental problems. Indeed, by transferring wealth from rich nations to poor, we are likely to create a new class of potential consumers, who, even if they are discouraged by our fair trade measures from stripping the wealth of other countries, may well strip the wealth of their own. There are of course plenty of international treaties governing issues such as habitat protection and the conservation of endangered species which the poor world's governments have freely signed and which, as a result, they should be encouraged to respect. But the rich world has no right to run other nations' economies at arm's length. Environmental decisions which have only local or national implications should surely be left to the people of the locality or the nation: how they handle their own resources is not a decision that other people should make. The fact that the people of developing nations will know, however, that no one else can be blamed for the destruction of their natural resources may well prove to be the catalyst for the development of a new environmental democracy. States will no longer be able to deny responsibility for the problem, while citizens will see that changing environmental policy no longer relies upon the improbable task of changing the behaviour of the governments and corporations of other nations.

Everyone on earth has a right, though, to lobby to prevent everyone else from generating pollution which crosses national borders, and from destroying the global resources – such as climatic stability and oceanic fisheries – on which the people of other nations depend. This, as the negotiations over the Kyoto protocol on climate change have shown, will never be easy, but the system suggested in this chapter has already generated a major incentive, through the need to purchase part of a nation's carbon quota, for the replacement of polluting technology with carbon-free development. Corporations investing in factories producing goods for export, which requires, under our system, the use of environmentally benign technology, are likely to use the same factories to produce goods for the domestic market.

You may have noticed that a conflict has developed between this proposal and the plan presented in the previous chapter for an International Clearing Union. If the aim of a Fair Trade Organization is to permit the poorer nations to catch up with the rich ones, then the poor nations must be permitted to sustain a trade surplus across several years. The rich nations would, between them, have to sustain a corresponding deficit. This is a possibility which the Clearing Union prevents. So the establishment of a Fair Trade

Organization must pre-date the establishment of an International Clearing Union.

Perhaps we are beginning, then, to see the development of a political programme. The first step would be to change the *rules* governing trade between nations, permitting a significant transfer of wealth from rich to poor. The second, once the poorer nations could compete on roughly equal terms, would be to address the *balance* of trade between nations, ensuring that temporary deficits did not contribute to permanent debt. The Clearing Union would then generate the money required for global elections and a world parliament. The parliament, in turn, can be used to examine and challenge the decisions made by the two other bodies, to hold them, in other words, to account. Political change is therefore preceded by economic change: by the time we are ready to start experimenting with global democracy, we may discover that as a result of redistribution and economic stabilization, our sense that we are locked in deadly competition with each other has already begun to diminish. Having almost reached the end of this manifesto, I realize that I've written it in reverse order.

None of the measures proposed in this book are sufficient, however, to address a far bigger question, that of the curtailment of the world-eating and mathematically impossible system we call capitalism, and its replacement with a benign and viable means of economic exchange. But I hope that, if implemented, they might begin to establish some of the preconditions in which a global debate about the world's economic and ecological destiny could begin. Because capitalism is built upon the lending of money at interest, capitalist economies are driven by the need to repay debt, which is why survival within this system is contingent upon endless growth. Endless growth is physically impossible.

As Heinrich Haussmann has shown, a single *pfennig* (about half a US cent) invested at five per cent compound interest in the year AD 0 would have yielded, by 1990, a volume of gold 134 billion times the weight of the planet.[154] Interest repayments, in other words, are feasible only in the short term. As debt can be paid only by generating value, capitalism seems destined to destroy the planet.

There may be another system – whose viability on a large scale has yet to be established – which does not depend upon net growth and which creates an ineluctable economic incentive for the conservation of resources. This system generates precisely the opposite pressures to those introduced by capitalism. To explain it and its implications in full would require another book, and this, I am relieved to say, has already been written, by the economics professor (and formerly the world's most successful currency trader) Bernard Lietaer.[155] But briefly, it works as follows. Rather than money gaining value over time through interest, it loses value, through *demurrage*, or negative interest. This means that it is impossible to invest in money, which is another way of saying that, if it could be universally applied, capitalism comes to an end.

Because the value of investment in real wealth (natural resources and productive capacity) under capitalism is judged against the value which could be gained from investing in money, capitalism ensures that businesses seek the most rapid of possible returns on their investment. If you can reap a return of ten per cent by investing in money, the money you invested in buying a forest, for example, will have lost almost all its comparative value within ten years. It is always more lucrative, therefore, to fell all the trees in the forest and sell them for timber than to preserve the forest for ever, felling only a few at a time. And if you *borrowed* the money to buy the trees, you will, if you are not to go bankrupt, need to repay it as soon as possible, by turning the natural wealth you have acquired back into money.

Demurrage ensures the opposite: the more slowly the investment matures, the less of your wealth is turned into money, so the less value it will lose. You will wish to extract only as much cash as you need to spend or want to transfer to another long-term investment. You will seek to sustain the value of the natural wealth you have acquired for as long as possible, and will curtail your spending accordingly. The entire economic system, in other words, could invest in the perpetuation of the planet.

While demurrage currencies have been applied to great effect at the level of the town or county during periods of economic crisis (in Austria, Germany and the United States during the early 1930s for example),[156] it is as yet far from clear that this system (or a series of such systems) would be globally applicable, or that the hazards of Lietaer's proposals would not outweigh the benefits. Some of their outcomes might conflict directly with our other objectives. But this, at least, is the scale on which we should be thinking, if we are serious about transforming the way the world works. It seems clear to me that such proposals belong to the second order of change. They will become feasible only when we have already begun to implement a system which strives towards equality.

What I mean by this is that it is impossible to establish common purpose between people whose economic lives vary as wildly as they do today. The ultra-rich will always regard the poor with terror, and the hatred which flows from terror. The extremely poor will always see the rich as a different species, placed upon the earth to govern and oppress them. Without a great global economic levelling, we are destined always to fight each other, rather than our common problems. So we encounter here a paradox: the proposals laid down in this chapter may permit us, through the deployment of a modified species of capitalism, to create the conditions in which capitalism can be destroyed.

*   *   *

All these plans will run immediately into the furious opposition of the rich world's corporations. They are likely to be
able to recruit not only their governments but also many
of the workers of the nations in which they are based. They
will argue that if their special protections (their intellectual
property rights, their ability to dump their costs on other
people, the subsidies they receive from the state) and their
special access to the economies of weaker nations are discon-
tinued, the trading position of the country in which they
are based will deteriorate. Working people are likely to
support the corporations' contention that if poor nations
are permitted to exclude, during their development phase,
certain goods produced by the rich nations, workers in the
rich world will lose their jobs. Labour movements will also
argue that the initially cheaper workforces of the poor world
are likely, while producing the same goods, to outcompete
them both globally and domestically, just as the motor and
electronics sectors in the Far East outcompeted them in the
second half of the twentieth century.*

   In all cases they will be correct. They will have encountered that fundamental but perpetually neglected law of
economics: that if some nations are enjoying a trade surplus,

---

* Of course, workers in a few sectors in the rich world, who produce
  goods that are bulky and perishable (such as fish, fruit and vegetables),
  will benefit from these changes as a result of the valuation of externalities.

others must be in deficit. Of course, the nations which are poor today will be permitted an inequality of opportunity only until they catch up with the rich world, after which they become subject to the same trade rules and, this programme suggests, the balancing mechanisms overseen by the International Clearing Union. But during the initial period, the rich world will suffer from trade deficits and the accumulation of debt. There is, however, a major difference between the assertion that these measures will damage the rich world's trading position and the assertion, often made by those who resist international redistribution, that they will irreparably damage the economy, lead to a *net* increase in unemployment and impoverish the workers of the rich world.

For centuries governments have justified the iniquity of their trading positions with the contention that it is necessary for the welfare of their own people; and for centuries they have presided serenely over a system which permits an elite to secure almost all the ensuing benefits. One has only to read Friedrich Engels' *The Condition of the Working Class in England*[157] to see what one hundred years of global economic dominance and 500 years of protectionism had done for the people of the world's most powerful trading nation. Today, thanks to the effectiveness of the labour and suffrage movements of the late nineteenth and twentieth centuries and an increasing economic reliance upon the service sector and specialized manufacturing, the workers of much of the rich world are permitted a marginally greater share of the wealth their nations steal from others, though in some countries, such as the United States, their position is now deteriorating. But governments in the West continue to blame trading conditions for their inability to improve the lives of their citizens. They continue, in other words, to mislead.

The governments of the rich world are in a far better position to stimulate domestic demand than the governments of the poor world. They fail to do so not because the means are unavailable, but because those means reside in the hands of the rich, and the rich are better represented and better heeded in government than the poor. There are two obvious means of boosting the domestic market and therefore preventing a nation with a weakened trading position from slipping into recession. One is to reduce the taxes levied upon the poor. The other is to increase the taxes levied upon the rich, and use the extra revenue to enhance public spending.

By lobbying for unfair trade, labour movements in the Western world absolve their governments from social reform, permitting them endlessly to defer the necessary redistribution of wealth within their own economies. Far from improving their long-term prospects, workers thereby condemn themselves to continued economic and political exclusion. A just world is one in which the labour forces of all nations recognize that they can no longer evade their own problems by demanding the exploitation of other people.

But the corporations, the governments and the workers of the rich world may not now be able to prevent these changes, even if they wanted to. Recognizing that the collapse of the trade agreement in Seattle in 1999 threatened the collapse of the World Trade Organization, and therefore the abandonment of international trade rules, the rich nations promised that the next trade talks, beginning in Qatar in 2001, would be a 'development round', whose primary purpose was to deliver benefits to poorer nations. That promise, like all those preceding it, has been broken, as corporate lobbies in the United States and the European Union have prevented either the acceptance or the implementation of most of the necessary reforms. The US, for example, responding to pressure from its pharmaceutical industry, has blocked a deal supported by every other member of the WTO, which would have permitted poor countries to override corporate patents in order to provide their people with cheap drugs. Both the US and the EU have failed to begin to dismantle their farm subsidy system: the US, soon after suggesting in Qatar that it would reduce subsidies, raised them by a further $180 billion across the next ten years. The governments of the poor world have realized at last that all they can expect from the rich world is lies. They have been left with no option but to fight back.

Unlike the other powerful international institutions, the World Trade Organization permits them, in principle, to resist. They must surely soon decide to pursue one of two courses of action. One is to demand a new, genuine, development round, controlled by them, in which Green Room meetings and all other truncations of joint decision-making are banned, and through which they might hope to turn the WTO into some kind of Fair Trade Organization. The other is to judge the WTO, as a result of corporate infiltration and the rigged appointment of its officers, to be inherently corrupt, and to break away and establish a Fair Trade Organization from scratch. There is, as they are now aware, no future for them in belonging to a trade organization which remains dominated by the rich minority.

We must hope that they are also beginning to recognize that they can no longer permit themselves to be picked off one by one, but must act with greater solidarity than they have been courageous enough to demonstrate so far. We might also hope that if they don't do it, their people will overthrow them and install governments which will.

The poor world has, therefore, three possible weapons at its disposal. The first is the *internationally* democratic structure of the World Trade Organization. The second is their combined power to break the WTO and establish an alternative organization. The third is the weapon whose dimensions were explored at the end of Chapter 5: international debt and the poor nations' consequent ownership of the banks. A fair trading system could be added to an International Clearing Union as a condition of refraining from a mass coordinated default.

None of the proposals suggested here solves all the problems associated with the regulation of international trade. We can expect the powerful nations to seek to enforce the same inequalities through regional agreements, and here too they will have to be resisted. We are left, as well, with the issue of the undemocratic nature of any gathering of states: the tiny nations, representing very few people, possess the same voting power as the biggest ones, while governments of all kinds make unmandated decisions on behalf of their people. Our world parliament provides a means of moderating their power, helping to ensure that both the states and the gathering of states are held to account by their citizens. But even if internationalism were to remain, in this respect, unamenable to globalization, a system based on the majority decisions of all states, irrespective of their wealth or history, comes closer to democracy than a decision made for everyone else by the Quad.

Those governments of the poor world which demand radical change need the support of global justice campaigners in the rich world. But, thanks to the pernicious impact of the localization agenda, some campaigners in the rich world have been perceived by the citizens of poor nations as their enemies. Campaigns whose overriding purpose is redistribution are campaigns whose solidarity with the poor world is immediate and unshakeable. They are campaigns which would take us a step closer to the metaphysical mutation.

CHAPTER 7

The Contingency of Power

If, having read the previous six chapters, you have concluded that 'something ought to be done', then I have succeeded in one respect, and failed in another. I may have convinced you that radical change is necessary, perhaps also that it is possible, even inevitable. But the measure of my failure is the placidity of your response. It costs nothing to agree that something should be done; indeed people like us have been accepting this proposition for decades, and waiting for someone else to act on it. Constitutional change will begin only when we reach the more dangerous conclusion that 'I must act'.

There have been many occasions over the past few years on which we have won the argument and lost the war. The campaigners who have exposed the injustices of the current global system often succeed in generating a widespread demand for change, and just as often discover that this demand has no outlet. Our opinions, in these circumstances, count for nothing until we act upon them. Until we present a direct constitutional challenge to its survival, or, through such measures as a threatened conditional default, alter the circumstances in which it operates, those who maintain the dictatorship of vested interests will read what we write and listen to what we say without the slightest sense of danger. In 1649, after recoiling from the satisfaction he felt upon completing one of his revolutionary pamphlets, Gerrard Winstanley noted 'my mind was not at rest, because nothing was acted, and . . . words and writings were all nothing, and must die, for action is the life of all, and if thou dost not act, thou dost nothing'.*[158] This manifesto, and all the publications like it, is worthless unless it provokes people to action.

There are several reasons why we do not act. In most cases, the personal risk involved in the early stages of struggle outweighs the potential material benefit. Those who catalyse revolution are seldom the people who profit from it. In this struggle, most of us are not yet directly confronting armed force (though this may well change as we become effective), so the risks to which we expose ourselves and our

---

* Winstanley then 'tooke my spade and went and broke the ground upon *George-Hill*', beginning one of the first and arguably the most ambitious of the post-mediaeval revolutionary movements in western Europe.

families are, as yet, slighter than those encountered by other revolutionaries. Nor, of course, are the potential benefits of resistance as obvious, for those activists who live in the rich world, as the benefits of overthrowing Nazi occupation or deposing an indigenous tyrant, or breaking away from a formally constituted empire. While most of the people of the poor world have an acute need to change the circumstances which govern the way they live, the problems the protesters in rich nations contest belong to the second order of concern: we are not confronted by imminent starvation or death through waterborne disease, but by distant wars, economic instability, climate change and the exhaustion of resources; issues which seldom present immediate threats to our survival.

But while the proposals in this manifesto offer little by way of material self-advancement to activists in the rich world, there is, in collective revolutionary action, something which appears to be missing from almost every other enterprise in modern secular life. It arises, I think, from the intensity of the relationships forged in a collective purpose concentrated by adversity. It is the *exultation* which Christians call 'joy', but which, in the dry discourse of secular politics, has no recognized equivalent. It is the drug for which, once sampled, you will pay any price.

All those with agency are confronted by a choice. We can use that agency to secure for ourselves a safe and comfortable existence. We can use our life, that one unrepeatable product of four billion years of serendipity and evolution, to earn a little more, to save a little more, to win the approval of our bosses and the envy of our neighbours. We can place upon our walls those tombstones which the living erect to themselves: the framed certificates of their acceptance into what Erich Fromm has called the 'necrophiliac' world of wealth and power.[159] We can, quite rationally, subordinate our desire for liberty to our desire for security. Or we can use our agency to change the world, and, in changing it, to change ourselves. We will die and be forgotten with no less certainty than those who sought to fend off death by enhancing their material presence on the earth, but we will live before we die through the extremes of feeling which comfort would deny us.

I do not presume to lecture those who have little agency – among them the majority who live in the poor world – on how to manage their lives. Over the past five years in many of the countries of the poor world – though this is seldom reported in the West – people have tried to change their circumstances through explosive demonstrations of grief, anger and hope. I have sought, with this manifesto, simply to enhance that hope, by demonstrating that there may be viable alternatives to the systems that subjugate them.

But for most of the people of the rich world, and the more prosperous people of the poor world, revolution offers the possibility of freedom from the constraints we impose upon ourselves. Freedom is the ability to act upon our beliefs. It expands, therefore, with the scope of the action we are prepared to contemplate. If we know that we will never act, we have no freedom: we will, for the rest of our lives, do as we are told. Almost everyone has some sense that other people should be treated as she would wish to be. Almost everyone, in other words, has a notion of justice, and for most people this notion, however formulated, sits somewhere close to the heart of their system of beliefs. If we do not act upon this sense of justice, we do not act upon one of our primary beliefs, and our freedom is restricted accordingly. To be truly free, in other words, we must be prepared to contemplate revolution.

Another reason why we do not act is that, from the days of our birth, we are immersed in the political situation into which we are born, and as a result we cannot imagine our way through it; we cannot envisage that it will ever come to an end. This is why imagination is the first qualification of the revolutionary. A revolutionary is someone who recognizes the contingency of power. What sustains coercive power is not force of arms, or even capital, but belief. When people cease to believe – to believe in it as they would believe in a god, in its omnipotence, its unassailability and its validity – and when they act upon that belief, an empire can collapse, almost overnight.

Those who possess power will surrender it only when they see that the costs – physical or psychological – of retaining it are higher than the costs of losing it. There have been many occasions on which rulers possessed the means of suppressing revolt – the necessary tanks and planes or cannons and cavalry divisions – but chose not to deploy them, because they perceived that the personal effort of retaining power outweighed the effort of relinquishing it. One of the surprises of history is the tendency of some of the most inflexible rulers suddenly to give up, for no evident material reason. They give up because they are tired, so tired that they can no longer sustain the burning purpose required to retain power. They are tired because they have had to struggle against the unbelief of their people, to reassert, through a supreme psychological effort, the validity of their power. We cannot rely on this desistance – many others have fought past the point of all reason, seeking to hold on to power even at the expense of their own lives – but it is one of those many psychological frailties which has always threatened the survival of the systems the powerful create for themselves. It is an infirmity whose symptoms we should be ready to detect.

There is something about our time which permits nothing to last for long. All the world's pre-existing empires collapsed in the twentieth century, and no formal imperial system established within that century outlived it. Some have interpreted this as the end of history, the definitive triumph of capitalism and its attendant ideology, market fundamentalism. But even this world order is already showing the classic signs of senescence. Its lieutenants have become obsessed with harvesting the fruits of office.* Its political class has been infected with bizarre religious beliefs.† Some of its most important agents – men such as George Soros and Joseph Stiglitz – have turned. The dictatorship of vested interests is succumbing to entropy.

We can hasten its collapse, but only if we are prepared to turn our intermittent campaigns into a sustained revolt. We must start to develop a strategic and systematic means of curtailing the Age of Coercion.

This process has now begun, with the passionate debates required to start to design a world order which reflects the will of the world's people. I hope this manifesto will contribute to these debates, if only because it might incite

---

* Executive pay packages in the United States, for example, rose by 77.7 per cent between 1997 and 2002.[160]
† One of the reasons why George Bush has refused to restrain Israel's treatment of the Palestinians is that his political allies in the Christian Coalition believe that the Rapture – the first stage of the Apocalypse – cannot begin until the Jews have taken possession of all the lands decreed by the Bible to be theirs, after which they will be converted to Christianity. By supporting Israel against Palestine, they believe they are hastening the Apocalypse, and hence their own exaltation. Tony and Cherie Blair, for their part, have indulged in some of the wildest excesses of New Age mysticism, from communing with the dead through a medium to smearing their naked bodies with mud and papaya before primal screaming in a Mexican temple.[161]

such revulsion that other people will feel obliged to quash it with better proposals of their own. But that we must have proposals, and that we must seek, before long, to provide a single, coherent programme of alternatives to the concentrated power of the dictatorship of vested interests, is surely evident. You might, with good reason, judge that I have not formulated such a programme, or that I have formulated the wrong one. But simply to reject it is insufficient. You must, as I have suggested, then replace it with a better one.

But let us assume, for the sake of this discussion, that having tested them against the alternatives, you decide that the proposals in this manifesto, or something resembling them, offer the best opportunity for achieving global justice. What, then, constitutes effective action?

We can set to work immediately on building the foundations for a world parliament. There is a necessary role here for hundreds of thousands of activists, in explaining the idea in their own nations and putative constituencies, in organizing the community consultations which would test the public response, in competing with the media bosses who are likely to seek to turn people against it. While the implementation of such a parliament will have to wait upon our other proposals, which would generate the money required to make it viable, there is no reason why we cannot begin the necessarily lengthy preparations.

Public pressure to dump the Security Council and pass its responsibilities to a democratised General Assembly will largely depend on the outcome of the war in Iraq. But it seems to me to be inevitable that the massive peace campaigns which have drawn so much of their strength from the global justice movement will begin before long to concentrate on the need for a new international security system, which protects us from the tyranny of the strong as well as the terrorism of the weak.

Nor do we need to wait for anyone's permission to start our campaigns for a Fair Trade Organization and an International Clearing Union. Dissidents in the poor world, if they adopt these proposals, could begin seeking to make the overthrow of the existing international systems – backed up by the threat of conditional default – their people's core political demand, in the hope that it starts to become the issue on which elections are won or lost. Activists in the rich world could support this campaign by promoting and explaining it, and continuing to press for the abolition of the old institutions, assisted by the fact that we may now have a far better system with which to replace them. We can use all the tactics we have deployed in the past – marches, demonstrations, non-violent direct action, letter-writing, petitioning, political lobbying – but with the confidence that we can explain not only what we don't want, but also what we do. We must continue to develop our alternative information networks, and to enhance too the use of the most effective and widespread of all media: word of mouth.

This does not mean that all those who wish to change the world by these means must immediately give up everything else they are doing. All successful movements engage both full-time and part-time activists. The full-time activists – often supported financially by the contributions of the part-timers – are responsible above all for the continuity and momentum of the campaigns, ensuring that they continue to develop even when they are out of the public eye. They will help the part-timers to be as effective as possible, and to avoid the duplication of effort. In turn, the part-timers must hold the full-timers to account, and help, through free-thinking and open discussion, to develop both the ideas towards which they work and the strategies they use to implement them. There are hundreds of such networks operating already within the global justice movement.

If such campaigns are to succeed, they need to call not only upon existing activists, but also upon many people who are not yet engaged in transformative politics. In most democratic nations, citizens are withdrawing from the political process. Mainstream politics has become, especially for young people, boring and alienating, as many correctly perceive that it has been reduced to a matter of management, that the competing parties in most nations have been captured by a class of people permitted by corporations and the financial markets to govern, whose aims and outlook are almost identical. There is no outlet, in most national systems, for passion. Globalization has increased the complexity of political issues and, by removing their resolution to levels at which there is no democratic control, exacerbated people's sense of helplessness.

The global justice movement has become, for many of those alienated from national politics, an enfranchisement movement. By lifting their sights from the national sphere to the global or international sphere, they have discovered that the potential for political engagement has not disappeared, but merely shifted to another realm. Older activists have rediscovered, in the extraordinary numbers these global campaigns have mustered, some of the hopes which have lain dormant for the past twenty years. By demonstrating that we have the means of both democratizing and transforming global politics, we can turn this movement – which is already the biggest global federation ever convened – into a force so numerous and so effective that it becomes irresistible.

But even if you accept the proposals promoted in this manifesto, you should see them as just one contribution to the process of debate and development. While I have concentrated on what I believe are some of the key issues in global governance, there are several I have not attempted properly to tackle. These include the denomination of countries' foreign exchange reserves and the global power of the dollar; the generation of debt by the commercial banks through the process known as 'fractional reserve banking'; and the erosion of the tax base, as companies shift their assets into countries which charge them less. These issues have already been addressed by other people.[162] So please do not regard this book as comprehensive. It could become part of the process of change, but only if other people improve, augment and develop its proposals.

All political systems are ephemeral, and we can expect any new means of governance we design to collapse eventually and be succeeded by others, perhaps even to age as rapidly as the deceased systems of the past century or so. But there is also a possibility that, rather than merely replacing one set of institutions with another, we might call forth something else, something much bigger, more menacing and more persistent: the metaphysical mutation which transforms the way in which human beings perceive themselves, and which nothing but another metaphysical mutation can halt. This transformation will not bring oppression to an end, or alter any of the basic human instincts which make us the flawed and dangerous creatures we are, but, if it occurs, it will establish a framework of perception which permits us to cooperate in resolving our common problems.

None of these upheavals will happen spontaneously. The existing institutions cannot reform themselves. Their power relies upon the injustice of the arrangements which gave rise to them, and to tackle that injustice would be to accept their own dissolution. Governments will not act on our behalf until we force them to do so. The political classes from which most governing parties are drawn have no interest in this revolution. This shift, in other words, depends not on an amorphous *them*, but on a specific *you*. It depends on your preparedness to abandon your attachment to the old world and start thinking like a citizen of the new; to exchange your security for liberty, your comfort for elation. It depends on your willingness to act.

Well? What are you waiting for?

References

All web addresses cited were current on 1 March 2003, unless otherwise specified.

1: Michel Houellebecq, 2001. *Atomised*. Vintage, London. First published in France as *Les Particules élémentaires*.
2: John Holloway, 2002. *Change the World Without Taking Power: The Meaning of Revolution Today*. Pluto Press, London.
3: See Articles 108 and 109 of the *Charter of the United Nations*.
4: IMF *Articles of Agreement*, page 84. http://www.imf.org/external/pubs/ft/aa/aa.pdf; World Bank members, e.g.: International Bank for Reconstruction and Development *Articles of Agreement: Article VIII*. http://web.worldbank.org/wbsite/external/extaboutus (About Us > Organization > Articles of Agreement); International Finance Corporation *Articles of Agreement: Article VII*. http://www.ifc.org/about/articles/article7/article7.html
5: IMF: *Members' Quotas and Voting Power, and IMF Governors*. http://www.imf.org/external/np/sec/memdir/members.htm World Bank: *Voting Power of Member Countries*. http://web.worldbank.org/wbsite/external/extaboutus/ (About Us > Organization > Executive Boards).

6: e.g. The Center for International Environmental Law, November 2002. *NGOs Call on Trade Ministers to Reject Exclusive Mini-Ministerials and Green Room Meetings in the Run-Up to, and at, the 5th WTO Ministerial: The 14–16 November mini-ministerial in Australia.* http://www.ciel.org/Tae/WTO_5Min_112002.html; Ngaire Woods and Amrita Narlikar, November 2001. 'Governance and the limits of accountability: the WTO, the IMF and the World Bank.' *The International Social Science Journal* No. 170; Aileen Kwa, 30–31 July 2001. 'Developing Countries In Despair Over WTO Preparations For Doha.' *Focus on the Global South,* Bangkok.

7: The World Bank, 2002. *World Development Report 2000/ 2001: Attacking Poverty.* World Bank Group, Washington DC.

8: United Nations Food and Agriculture Organization, 2002. *The State of Food Insecurity in the World 2002.* FAO, Rome.

9: The Organization for Economic Cooperation and Development, 2002. *Preparing for the World Summit: Some Information about Sustainable Development.* Compiled by Vangelis Vitalis. OECD, Paris.

10: ibid.

11: ibid.

12: Lester R. Brown, 1997. *The Agricultural Link: How Environmental Deterioration Could Disrupt Economic Progress.* Worldwatch Paper 136. The Worldwatch Institute, Washington DC.

13: L.M. Maene, 1999. *Phosphate Fertilizer Production, Consumption and Trade: The Present Situation and Outlook to 2010.* Paper presented to the Sulphur Institute's 17th Sulphur Phosphate Symposium, 17–19 January 1999, Boca Raton, Florida. L.M. Maene is the Director General of the International Fertilizer Industry Association, Paris. http://www.fertilizer.org/ifa/publicat/PDF/ 1999_biblio_54.pdf. The figure cited here is eighty years for 'world phosphate reserves'. The 'reserve base' (phosphate which is not currently economically exploitable, because the concentrations are too low or it is not extractable) would, if it became available, provide a further 240 years' use. This is notional, however: it includes dispersed deposits on the ocean floor.

14: Figure compiled from: Luisa Kroll with Lea Goldman, 2002. *The World's Billionaires*. http://www.forbes.com/home/2002/02/28/billionaires.html

15: The World Bank suggests that the cost is 'between $20 and $25 billion per year for all the health-related goals'. See: World Bank. *The Costs of Attaining the Millennium Development Goals*. http://www.worldbank.org/html/extdr/mdgassessment.pdf. The World Health Organization's Commission on Macroeconomics and Health estimates that $22 billion in extra foreign aid per annum is required by 2007, if recipient governments increase their contribution to health by about 1.5 per cent of GDP. Cited in the same World Bank paper.

16: US Census Bureau, 2002. *Statistical Abstract of the United States, Table 1350*. US Department of Commerce, Washington DC.

17: Romilly Greenhill and Ann Pettifor, April 2002. *The United States as an HIPC (Highly Indebted Prosperous Country) – how the poor are financing the rich*. Jubilee Research at the New Economics Foundation, London.

18: Karl Marx and Friedrich Engels, 1967. *The Communist Manifesto*. Penguin, London. This is Samuel Moore's translation of 1888. The *Manifesto* was first published in German in 1848.

19: ibid.

20: ibid.

21: This phrase was first used by Marx in his *Letter to Joseph Weydemeyer*, on 5 March 1852. First published in *Jungsozialistische Blätter*, 1930. Available in translation at http://www.marxists.org/archive/marx/works/1852/letters/52_03 05.htm

22: George Monbiot, 2003. *No Man's Land: an Investigative Journey through Kenya and Tanzania*. Green Books, Totnes, Devon. First published in 1994 by Macmillan, London.

23: Karl Marx, 1852. *The Eighteenth Brumaire of Louis Napoleon*. First published in *Die Revolution*, New York.

24: Colin Hines, 2000. *Localization: A Global Manifesto*. Earthscan, London.

25: ibid.

26: ibid.

27: David C. Korten, 2000. *The Post-Corporate World: Life after Capitalism*. Berrett-Koehler, San Francisco and Kumarian Press, West Hartford, Connecticut.

28: ibid.

29: ibid.

30: George Soros, 2002. *On Globalization*. Public Affairs, Oxford.

31: ibid.

32: ibid.

33: The Charter of the United Nations is available online at http://www.un.org/aboutun/charter/

34: Global Policy Forum, 2002. Cited in The United Nations Development Programme, *Human Development Report 2002*. UNDP, New York.

35: The operations conducted between 1948 and 2002 are listed by Gore Vidal, 2002. *Perpetual War for Perpetual Peace: How We Got to be so Hated – Causes of Conflict in the Last Empire*. Clairview, London. First published in 2002 by Thunder's Mouth Press/Nation Books, New York.

36: There is an interesting discussion of these issues in Heikki Patomäki, Teivo Teivainen and Mika Rönkkö, 2002. *Global Democracy Initiatives: the Art of the Possible*. The Network Institute for Global Democratization, Helsinki.

37: For details about the pressure applied to members of the OPCW, see George Monbiot, 'Chemical Coup d'état', 16 April 2002 and 'Diplomacy US Style', 23 April 2002, published in the *Guardian*. Also available on www.monbiot.com

38: See: The Inter-Parliamentary Union, http://www.ipu.org/english/home.htm

39: See: The e-parliament, http://www.e-parl.net. Forthcoming.

40: Thalif Deen, 1 October 2002. 'UN Credibility at Stake Over Iraq,

Warn Diplomats'. Inter Press Service News Agency, Washington.

41: www.aceproject.org/main/english/sm and www.australianpolit-ics.com/elections/1996/abcost.shtml

42: Hamish Macdonnell, 27 December 2002. 'Holyrood site costing more than Strasbourg's'. *Scotsman.*

43: Gardiner and Theobald's *10th Annual Survey of Global Construction,* published in *Building Magazine,* 22 March 2002.

44: www.news.scotsman.com/topics.cfm?page=2&tid=177.

45: Hilary Wainwright, March 2002. 'Globalise the Left'. *Red Pepper* magazine.

46: Paul Kingsnorth, 2003. *One No, Many Yeses: A Journey to the Heart of the Global Resistance Movement.* Simon and Schuster, London.

47: T.J. Cornell, 1995. *The Beginnings of Rome: Italy and Rome from the Bronze Age to the Punic Wars (C. 1000–264 BC).* Routledge, London. I am indebted to Eric Fern for bringing this example to my attention.

48: Gumisai Mutume, 23 March 2001. 'World Bank says it won't abide by World Commission on Dams: NGOs Lambast World Bank For Ignoring Dam Guidelines'. Inter Press Service News Agency, Washington.

49: Aubrey Meyer, 2000. *Contraction and Convergence: The Global Solution to Climate Change.* Schumacher Briefing No. 5. Published by Green Books on behalf of the Schumacher Society, Bristol.

50: Joseph S. Nye Jr, March/April 2002. 'Parliament of Dreams.' *Worldlink*: the magazine of the World Economic Forum.

51: ibid.

52: Darrell Addison Posey, 1987. *Alternatives to destruction – science of the Mebengokre.* Museu Paraense Goeldi; Susanna Hecht and Darrell Addison Posey, 1989. 'Preliminary results on soil management techniques of the Kayapó Indians.' *Advances in Economic Botany* No. 7; A.B. Anderson and Darrell Addison Posey, 1989. 'Management of a tropical scrub savannah by the Gorotire Kayapó of Brazil.' *Advances in Economic Botany* No. 7.

53: http://www.worldparliamentgov.net/

54: http://www.wcpagren.org/cnfdeart.dir/article5.html

55: http://www.wcpagren.org/how.html

56: George Monbiot, 2000. *Captive State: The Corporate Takeover of Britain.* Macmillan, London.

57: Max Hastings, 2002. *Editor: An Inside Story of Newspapers.* Macmillan, London.

58: ibid.

59: Paulo Freire, 1996. *Pedagogy of the Oppressed.* Penguin, London. First published by Continuum in 1970.

60: Tess Kingham, 10 June 2001. 'New MPs Beware: If You Think You Can Express an Opinion, Forget It.' *Independent.*

61: Charter 99, 1999. *The Charter for Global Democracy.* Charter 99, London.

62: Oxfam, 2003. *Debt Relief and Education Spending: Learning the Hard Way.* Oxfam, Oxford.

63: Joseph Stiglitz, 2002. *Globalization and its Discontents.* Allen Lane, London. First published in 2002 by W.W. Norton, New York.

64: ibid.

65: ibid.

66: ibid.

67: ibid.

68: ibid.

69: See for example World Rainforest Movement, Forest Peoples Programme and Environmental Defense, 19 June 2002. *World Bank's Proposed Policy Puts World's Forests at Risk.* http://www.environmentaldefense.org/documents/2144_JuneAppeal.pdf

70: Robert Naiman, Center for Economic and Policy Research, 23 July 2000. 'World Bank Keeps African Kids Out of School.' *Sunday Journal,* Metro DC.

71: ibid.

72: Mark Lynas, 19 October 1999. 'Africa's Hidden Killers.' *Daily Mail & Guardian,* Johannesburg.

73: Cited by Charles Abugre, June 2000. *Still Sapping The Poor: a Critique of IMF Poverty Reduction Strategies.* The World Development Movement, London.

74: Oxfam 2003, as above.

75: IMF: *IMF Members' Quotas and Voting Power, and IMF Governors.* http://www.imf.org/external/np/sec/memdir/members.htm

76: World Bank: *Voting Power of Member Countries.* http://web.worldbank.org/wbsite/external/extaboutus/ (About Us > Organization > Executive Boards).

77: IMF: *IMF Members' Quotas and Voting Power, and IMF Governors.* http://www.imf.org/external/np/sec/memdir/members.htm

78: World Bank: *Voting Power of Member Countries.* http://web.worldbank.org/wbsite/external/extaboutus/ (About Us > Organization > Executive Boards).

79: United Nations Development Programme, 2002. *Human Development Report 2002: Deepening Democracy in a Fragmented World.* UNDP, New York; *Financial Times,* 22 May 2001. Editorial comment: 'Fresh Blood at the Fund'.

80: World Bank: *At A Glance.* http://web.worldbank.org/wbsite/external/extaboutus.html (About Us > What is the World Bank? > At A Glance)

81: e.g. Bread for the World Institute. *World Bank Facts & Figures.* http://www.worldhunger.org/articles/global/debt/facts.htm

82: Henry K. Liu, 11 April 2002. 'US Dollar hegemony has got to go.' *Asia Times.*

83: Romilly Greenhill and Ann Pettifor, as above.

84: Steen Jorgensen, director of the World Bank's Social Development Department, 26 September 2000, in response to a question from England & Wales Green Party representative Vanessa Hall at a meeting between NGOs and the World Bank in Prague. Recorded by Spencer Fitz-Gibbon.

85: *National Catholic Reporter,* 22 December 2000. Editorial: 'Millions of the World's Children are Desperate.'

86: Guaicaipuro Cuautemoc, May 2000. 'Carta De Un Jefe Indio

A Los Gobiernos De Europa: La Verdadera Deuda Externa.' *Revista Renancer Indianista*, No. 7.

87: Andrew Simms and Romilly Greenhill, no date given. *Balancing the Other Budget: Proposals for Solving the Greater Debt Crisis – How Globalisation Creates Debt and Why the Rich Are in Debt to the Poor.* Jubilee Research at the New Economics Foundation, London. www.jubileeresearch.org/analysis/reports/43.pdf

88: John Lloyd, 2001. *The Protest Ethic: How the Anti-Globalisation Movement Challenges Social Democracy.* Demos, London.

89: Joseph Stiglitz, as above.

90: Michael Rowbotham, 2000. *Goodbye America! Globalisation, Debt and the Dollar Empire.* Jon Carpenter, Charlbury, Oxfordshire.

91: I have drawn this account from three main sources: Michael Rowbotham, as above; Robert Skidelsky, 2000. *John Maynard Keynes: Fighting for Britain 1937–1946.* Macmillan, London; and Armand van Dormael, 1978. *Bretton Woods: Birth of a Monetary System.* Macmillan, London.

92: Lord Robbins, cited in Armand van Dormael, 1978, as above.

93: Harry Dexter White, cited in Armand van Dormael, 1978, as above.

94: Lord Keynes, cited in Skidelsky, 2000, as above.

95: Harry Dexter White, cited in New Economics Foundation, 2000. *It's Democracy, Stupid: the trouble with the global economy – the United Nations' lost role and democratic reform of the IMF, World Bank and the World Trade Organisation.* NEF, World Vision and Charter 99.

96: Harry Dexter White, cited in Van Dormael, as above.

97: Van Dormael, as above.

98: ibid.

99: Robert Skidelsky, as above.

100: Lord Keynes, cited in Michael Rowbotham, as above.

101: Sir Edward Holloway, cited in Michael Rowbotham, as above.

102: Geoffrey Crowther, cited in Michael Rowbotham, as above.

103: *Economist*, 2002. *Pocket World in Figures 2003*. Profile Books, London.

104: The Organization for Economic Cooperation and Development, 2002, as above.

105: Oxfam International, 2002a. *Rigged Rules and Double Standards: Trade, Globalisation and the Fight Against Poverty*. Oxfam, Oxford.

106: ibid.

107: www.europa.eu.int/comm/agriculture/agrista/2001/table-en/ en3511.pdf; www1.oecd.org/scripts/cde/members/LFSDATA Authenticate.asp; www.cia.gov/cia/publications/factbook/ fields/2012.html; The Farm Accountancy Data Network; www.census.gov/statab/www/; www.sourceOECD.org

108: Oxfam International, 2002b. *Cultivating Poverty: The Impact of US Cotton Subsidies on Africa*. Oxfam Briefing Paper 30, Oxford.

109: Estimates by the International Cotton Advisory Committee, cited in Oxfam International, 2002b, as above.

110: OECD (2000), *Agricultural Policies in OECD Countries: Monitoring and Evaluation*, OECD, Paris records a value of $335 billion, to which I have added the extra $17 billion a year introduced by the new US package.

111: Kevin Watkins, 26 August 2002. 'Main development from WTO talks is a fine line in hypocrisy.' *Guardian*.

112: United Nations Conference on Trade and Development, 1999. *Report on Trade and Development*. UNCTAD, Geneva.

113: Mark Curtis, 2001. *Trade for Life: Making Trade Work for Poor People*. Christian Aid, London.

114: Oxfam International, 2002a, as above.

115: Mark Curtis, as above.

116: United Nations Conference on Trade and Development, 1997. *Trade and Investment Report 1997*. UNCTAD, Geneva.

117: Ha-Joon Chang, 2002. *Kicking Away the Ladder: Development Strategy in Historical Perspective*. Anthem Press, London.

118: ibid.

119: ibid.

120: ibid.

121: ibid.

122: ibid.

123: Mark Curtis, as above.

124: ibid.

125: John Brohman, April 1996. 'Postwar Development in the Asian NICs: Does the Neoliberal Model Fit Reality?' *Economic Geography*, Volume 72, Issue 2.

126: Takatoshi Ito, 1996. *Japan and the Asian Economies: a 'Miracle' in Transition*. Brookings Papers on Economic Activity, Issue 2. The Brookings Institution, Washington DC.

127: Graham Dunkley, 2000. *The Free Trade Adventure: The WTO, the Uruguay Round and Globalism*. Zed Books, London. First published in 1997 by Melbourne University Press.

128: Ha-Joon Chang, 2002, as above.

129: Robert Wade, 1990. *Governing the Market: Economic Theory and the Role of Government in East Asian Industrialization*. Princeton University Press.

130: Duncan Green, 11 September 2000. 'Allow More Tigers Out of Their Cages.' *Guardian*.

131: Ha-Joon Chang, 1994. *The Political Economy of Industrial Policy*. Macmillan, London.

132: *Economist*, as above.

133: Weisbrot et al., cited in Ha-Joon Chang, 2002, as above.

134: Greg Palast, 8 October 2000. 'An internal IMF study reveals the price "rescued" nations pay: dearer essentials, worse poverty and shorter lives.' *Observer*.

135: United Nations Development Programme, 2002. *Human Development Report 2002: Deepening Democracy in a Fragmented World*. UNDP, New York.

136: Analyses from five UN agencies, cited by Mark Curtis, as above.

137: United Nations Development Programme, 1997. *Human Development Report 1997: Human Development to Eradicate Poverty*. UNDP, New York.

138: Aileen Kwa, 19 October 2001. 'Crisis in WTO Talks!' *Focus on the Global South*, Bangkok.

139: Ha-Joon Chang, 2002, as above.

140: *Economist*, as above.

141: Eric Schiff, 1971. *Industrialisation Without National Patents: The Netherlands, 1869–1912; Switzerland, 1850–1907*. Princeton University Press. This is a fascinating account of the means by which these nations developed largely without intellectual property laws. Interestingly, some of the companies which benefited most from this approach (such as Nestlé, Unilever, Syngenta and Philips) are now among those which most fiercely defend their own patents.

142: Colin Hines, as above.

143: World Bank, 1993. Cited in John Brohman, as above.

144: *Economist*, as above.

145: Colin Hines, as above.

146: Clair Wilcox, 1949. *Charter for World Trade*. Macmillan, New York.

147: William Diebold Jr, 1952. 'The End of the ITO.' *Essays in International Finance* No. 16. Princeton University Department of Economics; John Odell and Barry Eichengreen, 1998. *The United States, the ITO and the WTO: Exit Options, Agent Slack, and Presidential Leadership*. In *The WTO as an International Organisation*, edited by Anne O. Krueger. University of Chicago Press.

148: All cited in Mark Curtis, as above.

149: AFL-CIO, 2001. *Position Paper on Global Conference*. http://staff.bath.ac.uk/hssgjr/simul/papers/afl-cio.pdf

150: International Labour Organization, 1977. *The Tripartite Declaration of Principles concerning Multinational Enterprises and Social Policy*. ILO, Geneva.

151: Drafted during the 52nd session of UNHCR's Subcommission on the Promotion and Protection of Human Rights, 1998–1999.

152: Organization for Economic Cooperation and Development, 2001. *Guidelines for Multinational Enterprises: Text, Commentary and Clarifications*. OECD, Paris.

153: Ralph Estes, 1996. *Tyranny of the Bottom Line: Why Corporations Make Good People Do Bad Things*, cited in David Korten, as above.

154: Heinrich Haussmann, 1990. *Die Josefpfennig.* Cited in Bernard Lietaer, 2001. *The Future of Money: Creating New Wealth, Work and a Wiser World.* Random House, London.

155: Bernard Lietaer, 2001. *The Future of Money.*

156: ibid.

157: Friedrich Engels, 1999. The Condition of the Working Class in England. Oxford University Press. First published in German in 1845.

158: Gerrard Winstanley, 1649. *A Watch-Word to the City of London and the Armie.* Giles Calvert, London. Reprinted in *Gerrard Winstanley, Selected Writings*, edited by Andrew Hopton, 1989. Aporia Press, London.

159: Erich Fromm, 1973. *The Anatomy of Human Destructiveness.* Holt, Rinehart and Winston, New York.

160: Economic Research Institute, 2002. www.eri-executive-compensation.com/PDF/PressReleaseDecember2002.pdf

161: Tom Baldwin, 15 December 2001. 'Tony Blair "Reborn" Under the "Sacred Serpent" in New Age Ceremony.' *The Times*; Nick Cohen, 31 March 2002. 'Primal therapy.' *Observer*; Nick Cohen, 8 December 2002. 'Ev'rybody must get stones.' *Observer.*

162: e.g. Henry K. Liu, 23 July 2002. 'China vs the Almighty Dollar.' *Asia Times*; Romilly Greenhill and Ann Pettifor, as above; James Robertson, 1998. *Transforming Economic Life: A Millennial Challenge.* Schumacher Briefing No. 1. Published by Green Books on behalf of the Schumacher Society, Bristol; James Robertson, November–December 2000. 'The Alternative Mansion House Speech.' *The Social Crediter*, Vol. 79, No. 6. The Social Credit Secretariat, Edinburgh; Michael Rowbotham, as above; Andrew Mold, 2001. *Paying a Fair Share? A proposal for Unitary Taxes on the Profits of Multinational Enterprises.* Instituto Complutense de Estudios Internacionales, Madrid.

P.S.

Ideas,
interviews
& features...

Q & A

What is your idea of perfect happiness?

Setting out to sea in a kayak.

What is your greatest fear?

That human beings are incapable of reacting
to a problem until it becomes acute.

Which living person do you most admire?

All the people I admire most are those who
never feature in the media, but who work
quietly for a better world. Curiously, for
someone who is fiercely critical of both the
Catholic Church and the idea of missionary
work, the two who come to mind first are
both Catholic missionaries: a man called Frei
Adolfo, with whom I worked in the northeast
of Brazil, and a man called Joe Haas, whom I
met in West Papua. Both had left comfortable
lives in Western Europe to work in
conditions of great hardship and fear, and
both put the material welfare of local people
above their spiritual welfare, defending
them, at great risk to themselves, from land
owners and government officials.

What objects do you always carry with you?

A notepad and a pen.

**What single thing would improve the
quality of your life?**

A self-replicator, so that I can be in two places
at the same time.

What is the most important lesson life has taught you?

That almost everything I was brought up to believe is untrue. I don't blame my parents for this – they were brought up with the same self-justificatory myths of the British middle classes. All nations, all classes, all tribes tell themselves stories that validate and centralize their existence. These stories are always false.

Which writer has had the greatest influence on your work?

Thomas Paine.

Which book do you wish you had written?

The Life of the Automobile by Ilya Ehrenburg. He was able to make a polemic read like a novel. The closest modern equivalent, I think, is Eric Schlosser, with his book *Fast Food Nation*.

What are you writing at the moment?

Just articles. I'm planning to visit about thirty countries to talk about *The Age of Consent*, so I won't have time to write another book for a while.

Top Ten
Favourite Reads

Selected Poems
John Clare

The beautiful and tragic work of Britain's most shamefully neglected poet. The poems first document his ecstatic engagement with the land, its people and its wildlife, and then, as the landscape is divided up and ripped apart by enclosure, the creeping madness that accompanies his despair at its destruction.

The Rights of Man
Thomas Paine

Paine is someone I would hate to have crossed: he lays about his opponents with devastating wit, while building his case for democracy in a way that remains captivating after 200 years. If I could write like him, I would be a very happy man.

Anna Karenina
Leo Tolstoy

Levin's scything of the hayfield is the crispest and most compelling description I've come across in any work of prose. Like all Tolstoy's novels, Anna Karenina breaks down a bit towards the end, but somehow manages to show us the lives of its people as if we are seeing them for ourselves, and hearing their words as voices inside our own heads.

An Insular Possession
Timothy Mo

This book forces you to keep asking yourself whether you are reading fiction or a remarkably well-researched history. It is, of course, both, and creates a world so real that it is hard not to believe that every incident happened.

Dead Souls
Nikolai Gogol

A mad, rambling, almost structureless, but
staggeringly brilliant novel, by a mad and
rambling man. Like Dostoevsky, Gogol
manages in some places precisely to capture a
human character in just a sentence or two –
look out for the description of the officials
banqueting on fish.

The Good Soldier Svejk
Jaroslav Harsek
Svejk is a conscripted soldier in the Austro-
Hungarian army who spends his time trying to
desert while showing the utmost loyalty to the
cause. It's a brilliant and very funny study on
how to get one up on the authorities while
pretending to co-operate.

Ulverton
Adam Thorpe

A difficult, intricate and beautiful book, which
describes a fictitious village through the
separate accounts of its inhabitants across 350
years. As it draws together their stories, it shows
how people try to place themselves in their land
and, in doing so, misinterpret the past.

War with the Newts
Karel Capek

A stunning satire on human greed. A sea
captain discovers a species of intelligent
marine newt and brings some back to
Europe. It isn't long before they're employed
to start reclaiming the land from the sea. But
soon the newts begin, literally, to turn the
tide against their masters.

Soil and Soul
Alastair McIntosh

One day, when the value of this book is finally recognized, it will transform our perception of ourselves, our history, and our surroundings, much as the work of Alice Miller and Sven Lindqvist has done. It is a first step towards the decolonization of the soul: the essential imaginative process we have to undergo if we are to save the world from the political and environmental catastrophes that threaten it.

The Future of Money
Bernard Lietaer

Lietaer was once the world's top currency trader, but stepped back to ponder what he and his colleagues were doing to the world, and how the global money supply could be designed to protect people's livelihoods and the environment, rather than destroying them. It is a brilliant, visionary book, which makes you itch to start applying some of his ideas.

What the Critics Said

'This is an extremely important book', urges Michael Meacher in the *Guardian*. 'Monbiot offers a searchingly rigorous analysis of the sources of American power and presents a package of proposals that would radically redraw the present world order ... If it is too radical for some, can they suggest lesser options that will produce the same improvement in world justice and prosperity? The floor is theirs.'

The *Sunday Tribune* recognizes 'a sense of revolutionary enthusiasm that shines through this book ... and in the end it is all about engagement – about igniting political action and creating new possibilities'. 'This book is a polemic as well as a manifesto,' agrees the *Financial Times*, acknowledging that 'the problems are not just about lack of democracy, inequity and wrong-headed institutions, but about fundamental attitudes to the natural world and the human place in it, including our measurement of wealth and well-being'. 'Whether or not one shares his view of what is politically possible', declares the *Independent*, '*The Age of Consent* is a bracing challenge to the complacency of all varieties of establishment thinking.'

The *Daily Telegraph* praises Monbiot's 'admirable attempt to open our minds to new possibilities and spheres of debate' and warns 'if, contrary to all metropolitan dinner party thinking, you still regard America as your friend, *The Age of Consent* is powerful stuff'. 'At last', cheers the *Independent on Sunday*, 'the global justice movement has found a vision as expansive and planet wide as that of the American neo-conservatives. Let the battle of the ideas commence.' ■

Debate

Roger Scruton discusses democracy with George Monbiot

Dear George,

Your book has illuminated many things for me. You show that there has been a steady migration of decision-making from accountable bodies to committees of self-selected predators. You show how the WTO advances the interests of these predators and how the UN systematically betrays the cause for which it was founded. You persuasively detail the way in which politics is being trivialized and its agenda usurped by the bureaucrats. You argue with authority, wit, and humanity, and we are all in your debt. In the recent debate in which we both took part on *open-Democracy.net* it was clear that your book has reshaped the question of transnational decision making, while hugely raising the intellectual level. So if I have criticisms to make, this is a tribute to your ability to make things so crystal clear.

My main worry concerns your proposal for a world parliament, to be filled by 'Tribunes of the people'. You are dismissive of what you call 'the irrational loyalties of nationhood', believing that human beings can achieve a more open and universal sympathy for their species. Now it is true that the loyalties of nationhood are not founded in reason, any more than the loyalties of family life. But they are not irrational. They stem from the natural love that we bear towards the place and the customs that formed us. Ordinary people in the West regard themselves as citizens of a shared republic, rather than subjects of a ruling power. In my view it is national loyalty that has made this possible. For national loyalty is territorial: it transcends ties of family, religion, race and kin, in order to attach itself to a homeland. Hence

It permits the emergence of a law defined over territory, rather than over tribe, race, or faith. National loyalties are precisely what we need in the modern world, if we are to sustain a secular rule of law in the face of the mafiosi and the religious fanatics.

Life in a democracy is hard. It requires us to live with people of whose opinions, actions, and lifestyle we may deeply disapprove. It requires us freely to accept laws that damage our interests. You can easily coerce people into accepting these things. But they *freely accept* them only when they have acquired a habit of obedience towards their elected governments. And that means a shared loyalty towards their fellow citizens, even those with whom they profoundly disagree. It is thanks to the nation state that this loyalty became a reality in modern times. The nation state is built on real and taken-for-granted sympathies that involve no imaginative strain, no ability for abstract thinking or refined aspirations in those who experience them. You do not tell us how such sympathies could arise at the transnational level. Of course, you and I might cultivate an abstract love for our species: but most people won't and can't.

You rightly invite your critics to propose something better than the arrangement you defend, and you force me to recognize that I have no genuine answer. I doubt the possibility or desirability of global democracy. But I believe that accountability can be achieved without it. The common law of England is based on the right of the injured party to petition for a remedy. It has made powerful people answerable to those whom they oppress, even though common-law judges are not elected, and common law is never put to the vote. This suggests another way to global justice. What is wrong with the people who are destroying our planet is not that they were not elected but that they are not obliged to remedy the destruction that they cause. The principal

> ❝ Life in a democracy is hard. It requires us to live with people of whose opinions, actions, and lifestyle we may deeply disapprove. ❞

victims are the generations who will inherit the earth. I therefore see the problem rather as Burke saw the problem of government within the nation state: how to make decision-makers answerable to those who have no vote, since they are not yet born. And, like Burke, I don't think you answer the problem merely by giving more votes to the living.

Here I would like to make a plea on behalf of conservatism, since I believe it is the input that is principally missing from your argument. I admire the way in which you distance yourself from the Marxist and anarchist utopias, recognizing the opportunity that utopia offers to oppressive elites. But you retain the old leftist insistence on dividing humanity into two antagonistic factions: the rich, powerful oppressors, and the poor, weak oppressed. By doing this you make things look far simpler than they are: as though it were enough to 'empower' those who are poor and to thwart those who have made them so. It is false to suggest that, wherever there are rich and poor, the wealth of the one causes the poverty of the other. Moreover there are rich people without power, powerful people who do not oppress, and weak people who are also oppressors. There are people who are neither poor nor rich, with a bit of power, and who have no desire whatsoever to oppress – you and I, for instance. The task that lies before us is not to empower one group against another, but to achieve a new consensus in which all the many interests that are at large in modern society can converge on a common policy. To dichotomize is to privilege resentment, to undermine compromise, and to appear as an enemy of some of us when really you are the friend of all.

Dear Roger,

Thank you very much for your thoughtful and provocative response. Like everything you write,

> 6 It is false to suggest that, wherever there are rich and poor, the wealth of the one causes the poverty of the other. 9

it has forced me to think hard about my own position.

I think it is worth pointing out that the world parliament proposal is not in itself a direct assault upon the nation states. Its immediate purpose is to democratize the powers that nations have already ceded to global or international bodies, rather than to wrest still more powers from them.

But it is true to say that I hope the democratization of global governance might one day help us to overcome the loyalties of nationhood. Your defence of the nation state is a strong one, but I would counter that the loyalties it commands have not, in most cases, developed organically. Those who built nations – whether colonists, warlords, or liberators – had to work hard to persuade people that their sympathies should be confined to the borders they had established, rather than to either a smaller unit (tribe or clan) or a bigger one (empire or planet). They invented flags, national anthems, and oaths of loyalty. They dehumanized the people who lived beyond their borders. They waged wars against those whose fealty to the tribal or imperial leadership took precedence over their fealty to the kingdom or the republic.

The sympathies of some of those who live in long-established nations might now be 'taken-for-granted' and require 'no imaginative strain', but that was surely not the case during their formation, and it is surely not the case in many of the newer nations today. Does it really require more imaginative strain to recognize the commonality of humankind than to see the human beings on one side of an arbitrary line as allies, and those on the other as enemies? Does not the rapid dissolution of national distinctiveness and the backlash of ethnic cleansing and the persecution of immigrants suggest that the imaginative strain of nationhood is now becoming, in many parts of the world, almost unbearable?

I believe that a process rather similar (though less violent) to the formation of the nation state is now taking place at the global level. The corporate advertisers are seeking to persuade us all to eat Big Macs, drink Coca-Cola, and watch *Terminator II*. We might lament their remarkable success, but this success reveals that our loyalties and our identities remain malleable: most children with access to television can surely recite half a dozen advertising jingles with more confidence than they can sing their national anthem.

We have, in other words, begun to acquire new habits of obedience. At present we are, at the global level, the subjects of ruling powers rather than citizens of a shared republic. But is not the history of almost all democracies the story of a transition from the first state to the second? What, then, are the special impediments that prevent this transition from taking place at the global level?

You are of course right to state that *merely* giving more votes to the living cannot solve all the problems of governance, but it is surely one of the necessary steps. While there is, as you suggest, an urgent need for the living to be held accountable to the unborn, there is also a need, as Thomas Paine argued, for the living to be released from the power of the dead. Those who established the current world order are, in Paine's words, 'governing beyond the grave', as we have no legitimate means of amending the global constitution they constructed.

While it is true to say that most wealthy people have not contributed directly to the immiseration of the poor, I think it is also clear that the wealth of the rich nations is intimately associated with the poverty of the poor ones. Had Britain not destroyed the textile industries of India and Ireland, for example, it is hard to see how we could have secured our own industrial dominance. Today the rules imposed by the International Monetary Fund and the World

> ❛ *Merely* giving more votes to the living cannot solve all the problems of governance, but it is surely one of the necessary steps. ❜

Trade Organization ensure that the rich world can exploit the economies of the poor world far more effectively than the poor can exploit the rich. Financial speculators from the West, for example, can storm the vaults of weaker nations, with the result that millions are thrown out of work. Neither you nor I are responsible for this, and yet, in ways that are not always visible to us – as the plundered wealth is dispersed through our national economy – we benefit from it.

Dear George,

Your response is very hard to answer. I have to agree that the nation states have already ceded massive powers to international bodies, and that they cannot easily recuperate them. So, as you rightly imply, the question is how to control those powers, so that they are exercised in the common interest. You believe in a system of democratic representation as the best, maybe the only, alternative. And you further believe that the kind of global citizenship and transnational loyalty that will be needed for people to participate in the project and accept its verdicts will come about in time, maybe even replacing the (in your view) frequently highly artificial and transitional national loyalties. The cogency of that position is enhanced by many things that we witness in the world today – and especially by the seeming fragility of national governments, and by their unwillingness to resist the migration of their powers to unaccountable bodies.

Nevertheless, I do not see a global parliament as a feasible alternative. Its members would represent constituencies so vast as to be incapable of real representation. As for democratic accountability, I see little hope of achieving this at the global level until we have achieved it at the local level. It is precisely because so many of the seats at the UN are occupied by people who are not accountable to those in whose name they speak that the institution has failed. The same is true, incidentally, of the WTO, the UN Commission on Human Rights, and the ILO.

That is why I would advocate jurisdiction, rather than parliamentary legislation, as the way forward. We should establish institutions that have the power to offer remedies to those who are damaged by predation. I recognize that there are dangers here. As we know from American litigation, people can use the courts, too, as an instrument of predation. But a court with the power to compensate genuine petitioners for genuine damage would offer far more effective control over multinational corporations than a parliament most of whose members would be, in due course, ex-CEOs of multinational corporations. It would also permit the control of the self-selected NGOs who claim to represent us.

But this embryonic scheme is, I admit, only a suggestion for an answer. It is largely thanks to your work that we are beginning, now, to understand the question.

Best wishes,
Roger

Dear Roger,

Many thanks again for your excellent points. I agree that there is a problem with the idea of democracy at the global level. In our debate on *openDemocracy.net*, the author Paul Kingsnorth suggested that 'real democracy can only operate on a relatively small scale'. I think, by and large, he is right. The bigger the constituencies, the more remote, geographically and socially, our representatives become, and the fainter the voice of any one of their constituents. This is, as you suggest, already an impediment to 'real' democracy at the national and the European level. It will certainly be an impediment at the global level.

> ❛ The bigger the constituencies, the more remote, geographically and socially, our representatives become, and the fainter the voice of any one of their constituents. ❜

But the problem we have is this: that lurking behind everything said and done by the global justice movements is a presumption of representation. I have just returned from the second European Social Forum in Paris. It was an extraordinary event: 51,000 people discussed everything from Agriculture to Xenophobia. But we appeared to begin with the assumption that we were speaking on behalf of everyone. Looking around the meetings, I saw that this could not possibly be the case: most of the delegates were white, under thirty, and (because they could not have attended without them) in possession of time, money, and passports.

The men who run the institutions we confront can claim that we do not represent the wishes of the world's people and, for all we know, they may be right. The danger of self-appointment is that those who are voiceless today remain voiceless. Representative democracy, clumsy and incomplete as it is when applied at the global scale, seems to me to be the only means by which the majority would have some opportunity to be heard. It would be far from perfect, but surely less imperfect than all the alternatives, which give them no voice at all.

But this is not to say that it should be the only means of holding power to account, and I think judicial methods of the kind you suggest are essential. Perhaps we could envisage an expansion of the mandate of the International Criminal Court, permitting it to prosecute corporate executives as well as soldiers and politicians. But when a system possesses a bureaucracy and a judiciary, is there not something missing? If it is to represent something other than just the people who run it, should it not also possess a parliament?

With my best wishes,
George

Have You Read?

Captive State: The Corporate Takeover of Britain

Monbiot's bestselling exposé of how our society has been overcome by unaccountable corporate control and corrupt government, with disastrous results for local communities and for democracy itself.

'This book, politically speaking, is essential ... Did I say "essential" earlier? I meant "compulsory".'

NICHOLAS LEZARD, *Guardian*

Poisoned Arrows

An investigative journey through the forbidden lands of West Papua, the 2003 reissue has a new introduction by the author.

'Monbiot is fascinating about the forest, the birds, the plants and, above all, the people. Monbiot is a man one would be proud to travel with. Perhaps it's that which makes it a good travel book.' *Sunday Telegraph*

No Man's Land

An investigative journey through Kenya and Tanzania.

'George Monbiot has already done more to change the world and our perception of it than most of us can hope to achieve in a lifetime ... Now he has exposed what is going on in Kenya and Tanzania, where the nomadic people are being driven off their land and systematically murdered ... We need people like Monbiot more than ever before.' *New Scientist*

If You Loved This,
You'll Like...

No Logo *by Naomi Klein*
Detailed and impassioned call to arms,
exposing the ravages of globalization and
documenting the rise of protest around the
world.

....

Fast Food Nation *by Eric Schlosser*
Schlosser's disturbing and timely exploration
of one of the world's most controversial
industries. Fast food is so ubiquitous that it
now seems harmless. But the industry's drive
for consolidation, homogenization, and
speediness has radically transformed the
West's diet, landscape, economy, and workforce, often in insidiously destructive ways.

....

Globalization and its Discontents *by Joseph
E. Stiglitz*
Stiglitz, a former Chief Economist at the
World Bank, explains the functions and
powers of the main institutions that govern
globalization – the International Monetary
Fund, the World Bank, and the World Trade
Organization – along with the ramifications,
both good and bad, of their policies.

....

**Stupid White Men ... and Other Sorry
Excuses for the State of the Nation**
by Michael Moore

American satirist's entertaining rant on
Bush, racism, the culture of corrupt
capitalism, and the general state of his home
nation. Entertaining, outrageous, and
thought-provoking.

A Problem From Hell *by Samantha Power*
Pulitzer prize-winning exposé of the West's
involvement (or lack of involvement) in the
world's major conflicts and genocides.

....

**Rogue State: A Guide to the World's Only
Superpower** *by William Blum*
William Blum investigates the idea of the
'American Empire', showing that encounters
between the USA and other nations have
often been of the cruellest kind.

The Web Detective

www.monbiot.com
Monbiot's comprehensive website, with all
his journalism, essays, debates, background
information, and advice.

www.globalrising.org
A new site organized by Monbiot, whose
purpose is to answer the question everyone
who has read the book seems to ask him:
'What can I do?' It's a worldwide directory
of the progressive organizations involved in
positive global justice initiatives, in which
volunteer activists can play a meaningful
role. For every listing, the site provides
contact details, a brief description of what
the organization does, and of the kind of
voluntary help it could use.

www.openDemocracy.net
An online global magazine of politics and
culture, dedicated to 'free thinking for a free
world'.

www.worldcitizen.org
The website of the World Citizen Foundation,
one of the most effective organisations
pressing for a world parliament.

www.nigd.org
The Network Institute for Global Democratization has published some of the most
interesting material on democratic global
governance and the obstacles it encounters.

www.charter99.org
Calls for greater accountability and
transparency in global decision-making.

www.gatt.org
A brilliant spoof of the World Trade
Organisation, exposing the underlying
agenda of the powerful states.

www.oneworld.net
The news of the developing world which
doesn't reach the mainstream media.

www.brettonwoodsproject.org
Provides critical scrutiny of the World Bank
and IMF.

www.focusweb.org
The website of the developing country
network Focus on the Global South.

www.thecornerhouse.org.uk
Some fascinating essays on social justice and
environmental issues.

www.corporatewatch.org
A British campaign site monitoring the
excesses of corporate power.

www.corpwatch.org
The US equivalent of Britain's CorporateWatch.

BOOKSHOP

Now you can buy any of these great paperbacks from HarperCollins at **10%** off recommended retail price. **FREE** postage and packing in the UK.

A Problem from Hell
Samantha Power 0-00-717299-0   £9.99

No Logo
Naomi Klein 0-00-653040-0   £8.99

Fences and Windows
Naomi Klein 0-00-715047-4   £8.99

An Ordinary Person's Guide to Empire
Arundhati Roy 0-00-718163-9   £8.99

The Algebra of Infinite Justice
Arundhati Roy 0-00-714949-2   £8.99

Reading Lolita in Tehran
Azar Nafisi 0-00-717848-4   £7.99

Bringing Home the Revolution
Jonathan Freedland 1-84115-021-5   £6.99

Total cost _____

10% discount _____

Final total _____

To purchase by Visa/Mastercard/Switch simply call **08707 871724** or fax on **08707 871725**

To pay by cheque, send a copy of this form with a cheque made payable to 'HarperCollins Publishers' to: Mail Order Dept. (Ref: BOB4), HarperCollins Publishers, Westerhill Road, Bishopbriggs, G64 2QT, making sure to include your full name, postal address and phone number.

From time to time HarperCollins may wish to use your personal data to send you details of other HarperCollins publications and offers. If you wish to receive information on other HarperCollins publications and offers please tick this box ☐

Do not send cash or currency. Prices correct at time of press. Prices and availability are subject to change without notice. Delivery overseas and to Ireland incurs a £2 per book postage and packing charge.

20